Introduction

Reading Paper

Shakespeare Paper

Writing Paper

The Essentials of Key Stage 3 English covers all the skills and material which are externally assessed at Key Stage 3. It provides all the information pupils need in order to pass the National Curriculum Tests for English.

In Year 9, pupils will sit three test papers. The book is divided up into three corresponding sections to allow students to prepare for each paper separately.

Each section in the guide (identified by its symbol, alongside) begins by clarifying the nature of that particular test paper, including the time allowed and marks allocated to each question, the skills that are being assessed and what the examiners will be looking for in the pupils' answers.

The Reading Paper section concentrates on how to identify features of different types of writing and analyse texts. The section on the Shakespeare Paper looks at the four assessment focuses and how to tackle the different styles of questions that might arise in the test. The Writing Paper section explores different types of writing and gives advice on how to produce appropriate pieces in the test.

At the end of the Reading Paper and Writing Paper sections, and throughout the Shakespeare Paper section, there are test-style questions and annotated model answers. This is to familiarise pupils with the types of questions they will be asked in the test and to give them guidance on how they should go about answering them. It is inadvisable for pupils to try and reproduce these answers in the test.

A companion workbook, The Essentials of Key Stage 3 English Workbook is available. It comprises questions and activities to help pupils prepare for the tests and practise their skills.

The Essentials of Key Stage 3 English has been written by an expert team of English teachers / examiners, with over 60 years' teaching experience between them: Paul Burns, Jan Edge and Philippa Ronan. Their experience as examiners means that they have an excellent understanding of the criteria used for marking English papers and are able to offer invaluable advice on how to succeed in the test.

Contents

Test Overview

The Papers

The National Curriculum Tests for English at Key Stage 3 consist of three papers:

- **Reading Paper** – 1 hour 15 minutes, 32 marks
- **Shakespeare Paper** – 45 minutes, 18 marks
- **Writing Paper** – 1 hour 15 minutes, 50 marks.

Read The Questions

Read the test paper and each question very carefully. Underline key words in the questions to focus your mind and to help you understand exactly what the question is asking you to do before you begin to answer it.

Plan and Check Your Answers

In the Writing Paper you are given time to plan your answers, but it is also very important and very beneficial to plan your answers in the other papers too. A plan reminds you to structure your work in paragraphs, and helps you to produce a good answer which is clear, logical and flows well.

It is equally as important to check your work. Read it through and ensure you have covered everything you wanted to. Check your spelling and punctuation – it is easy to make mistakes when you are under pressure.

Revision Tips

- Read over some of the work you have done in school (especially work done under test conditions) and think about how it could be improved. Identify errors that you frequently make and practise until you no longer make them.
- Learn the terms for the language techniques listed on p.16–17 – what they describe, how and why they are used, and how the terms are spelt.
- Read all the test-style questions and the annotated model answers in the Shakespeare section. They will help you to prepare for a question on any assessment focus.

The information in this revision guide is not intended to replace what you have learnt in class. It just provides you with key points to help you revise.

Most importantly, try to stay calm in the test and enjoy writing your answers. Make the most of the chance to express yourself.

English test

En
KEY STAGE 3
LEVELS 4–7
2005

Reading paper answer booklet

First name _____
Last name _____
School _____

- The paper is **1 hour 15 minutes** long.
- You have **15 minutes** to read the Reading booklet before answering the questions in your answer booklet. During this time you should not open your answer booklet.
- You then have **1 hour** to write your answers.
- Write your answers in this booklet. You may ask for more paper if you need it.
- There are 14 questions totalling 32 marks on this paper.

For marker's use only.

	Tick
Borderline check (reading – including Shakespeare task)	

English test

En
KEY STAGE 3
LEVELS 4–7
2005

Shakespeare paper: *Richard III*

Please read this page, but do not open the booklet until your teacher tells you to start.

Write your name, the name of your school and the title of the play you have studied on the cover of your answer booklet.

This booklet contains one task which assesses your reading and understanding of *Richard III* and has 18 marks.

You have **45 minutes** to complete this task.

English test

En
KEY STAGE 3
LEVELS 4–7
2005

Writing paper

Please read this page, but do not open the booklet until your teacher tells you to start.

Write your name and the name of your school on the front cover of your answer booklet.

- This test is **1 hour and 15 minutes** long.
- You should spend: **45 minutes** on Section A: longer writing task
  30 minutes on Section B: shorter writing task
- You may spend the first **15 minutes** planning your answer to Section A on the planning page provided.
- Section A, the longer writing task, has 30 marks.
- Section B, the shorter writing task, has 20 marks.

The Reading Paper

Important Information

About the Reading Paper

- It tests your reading skills.
- It lasts for 1 hour and 15 minutes.
- There are 32 marks available.

This paper is designed to test your ability to read, understand and interpret a variety of texts.

In the test you will be given a booklet containing three pieces of writing. The texts may be from any type of writing and be about any subject. You will have 15 minutes to read through the booklet. The answer booklet will have questions to test your understanding of each extract. You are not permitted to open the answer booklet until you are told to do so. Once you have been told you can open the answer booklet you will have 1 hour to write your answers.

What are the Examiners Looking For?

The examiners are looking for you to...

- show that you understand the texts
- collect information or ideas from the texts
- use the **PEE** technique (you may call it something different):
  - make a **P**oint
  - provide **E**vidence (a quotation)
  - give an **E**xplanation for the point you have made
- show that you have understood things that might not be stated obviously in the text (i.e. that you can pick up ideas from what you have read)
- write about the style of the texts – the words, phrases and sentences that the writers have used and how they affect the reader (i.e. what they make the reader think or feel)
- write about the literary techniques (e.g. imagery) that the writers have used
- show that you are aware of the audience of the texts
- show that you understand the purpose of the text:
  - to entertain (e.g. a novel)
  - to persuade (e.g. an advert or charity leaflet)
  - to inform / instruct (e.g. a factual account)
- write about the writer's point of view (i.e. what the writer thinks about the topic).

About this Section of the Revision Guide

This section of the revision guide will cover each of the types of writing and explain how you can recognise them by spotting key features. It provides you with the technical terms you will need to learn, and looks at how to read the test questions and pick out the information you need to be able to answer the question.

English test

En

KEY STAGE
3

LEVELS
4–7

2005

Reading paper answer booklet

First name _____

Last name _____

School _____

- The paper is 1 hour 15 minutes long.
- You have **15 minutes** to read the Reading booklet before answering the questions in your answer booklet. During this time you should not open your answer booklet.
- You then have **1 hour** to write your answers. Write your answers in this booklet. You may ask for more

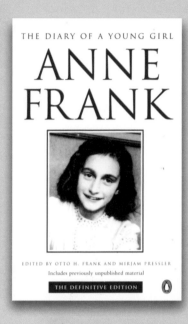

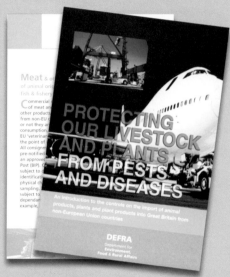

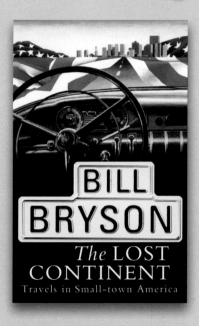

Test Guidance

Always read the question carefully. What are you being asked to do? Look at the marks available and the amount of space you have been given to write your answer: will a one-word answer be all right, or do you need to give an explanation? Are you being asked to find information from the text or to suggest reasons for the language that has been used? etc. When you are answering the questions in the test, always re-read the relevant part of the extract, don't just try to remember what it said.

Finding Links

There will be a link between the extracts you are given in the test paper. It helps to find the link between the texts when you are reading through them. The link could be…

- the subject or theme of the texts
- the audience they are aimed at
- the purpose of the texts
- the type (or genre) of text
- features of their style – the way that they are written and the words used.

Types of Writing

The three extracts that you get in the test can be from any sort of writing. Looking for features of the writing will help you to identify which genres the texts belong to.

A text can be categorised as **fiction**, which is concerned with imaginary people and events, or **non-fiction**, which is fact-based text. This distinction is easy to spot.

Writing can also be classified as **literary** or **non-literary** – this relates to the type of language and style used. This is not so clear cut because what exactly makes a piece of work literary can be debated.

This table gives you a rough guide to how different types of writing can be categorised. But remember, this is not set in stone.

	Fiction	**Non-fiction**
Literary	- Novels - Short stories	- Biographies - Travelogues
Non-literary	- Short stories - Pulp novels (Mills and Boon, etc.)	- Newspapers - Information leaflets - Text books

Punctuation

The way that a writer uses **punctuation** can be very important to the overall impact of the text on the reader. The punctuation marks are explained below.

Full stops . are found at the end of a sentence.
e.g. He didn't know what to do. He could see the man ahead. He must move.

Commas , are used in lists, and to punctuate long sentences by separating clauses (see p.11) which contain additional information.
e.g. The man, slowly removing the gun from its holder, faced his enemy, knowing that this might be his only chance for revenge.

Semi-colons ; are often used to join together two independent clauses; in other words, it joins two clauses that could be sentences. They can also be used to highlight a contrast.
e.g. Meg drives a Porsche; Dave drives a Ford van.

Colons : can be used to introduce a long list of things.
e.g. You will need to bring three things: a sleeping bag, a waterproof tent and a freeze box.

Exclamation marks ! can be used to show strong emotions, such as anger, surprise or excitement, or to show that a character is shouting.
e.g. Kelly's mother shouted 'Have you not tidied that bedroom yet? I asked you to do it yesterday!'

Question marks ? are used at the end of a direct question. People in power, e.g. police officers and judges, ask lots of questions. They can be used to show that a character is inquisitive (wants to know things) or is confused.
e.g. 'Why? What have I done wrong?'

Rhetorical questions are another form of direct question so they also have a question mark. They can be used in persuasive writing to make the reader think about the issue being addressed.
e.g. Do you think this is right?

Dashes – can be used to separate a strong interruption from the rest of a sentence.
e.g. The boys were playing irresponsibly – there was no other word for it – by the side of the road.

Ellipsis ... can be used to show pauses or to keep the reader in suspense.
e.g. She waited... and waited... and waited.

Brackets (parentheses) can go around explanations of words. They are used to contain additional material that could be removed from the sentence without destroying the meaning or flow.
e.g. Tony Blair (the leader of the Labour Party) attended an important meeting in Brussels yesterday.

Structure and Presentation

The **structure** of the text is how it is built up: what comes first, what is in the middle and how it ends.

You will be expected to explain what structure the author has used and why the author has chosen that particular structure. Some reasons could be…
- to present information in a clear and logical order
- to create suspense
- to make the narrative more enjoyable
- to give further information (flashbacks can be used for this reason).

The way in which the text is **presented** is also important.

What to Look For

In the test you should look at…
- the words used in the title of the text and how they are presented (font size, colour, etc.)
- the words used in the opening line and the type of sentence it is
- the layout of the text on the page (i.e. is it in paragraphs or columns, or set out in any other unusual way?)
- presentational devices, like bullet points
- formatting features in the passage (bold, italic, underlining, etc.)
- the way ideas are expressed throughout the passage (i.e. does the tone of the writing change?)
- the use of subheadings to separate sections of the text
- the use of pictures, graphs and/or diagrams
- the end of the passage; the final paragraph or the final line.

Extract from *The Unwelcome Surprise*

It was a beautiful day and Thomas had never been so happy. He would have his mother and father together again for the first time since their journey. He could see the trees swaying outside his window; it seemed as if they were waving a welcome home. Suddenly, he felt a shiver run through his body. A dark cloud covered the sun and his room felt cold and unwelcoming . He ran downstairs as quickly as he could, without looking back.

Using the 'what to look for' list, here are some points you could make about the extract.

- The title of the extract includes the word 'unwelcome' which suggests that something will happen that the boy is not happy about.
- The opening line is a short statement that is sufficient to set the scene.
- The text is a single paragraph with no special formatting.
- The diction (words) starts off being positive and happy (see orange highlighting), but then changes to words full of threat (see blue highlighting) and the words emphasise the uneasy atmosphere created. The tone of the passage changes due to the diction that has been used. The passage starts to sound threatening and a little scary.
- The passage ends leaving the reader with a chilling feeling that something bad is about to happen.

Analysing the Text

When you are writing about a text and commenting on its style you need to think about the text on three levels:
- word
- sentence
- whole text.

Analysing Words

At this level you need to look at…
- what words and phrases are used
- where the word is positioned in the text
- how the word is presented (e.g. use of font size, colour, italics, etc).

What words are used and what effect do these words have on the reader? Don't forget to use the terms that have been covered so far. Look at this example:
The defenceless puppy lay whimpering in the corner.

The **adjective** 'defenceless' makes the puppy appear weak and vulnerable and the **verb** 'whimpering' makes the reader feel sorry for the puppy because it is making a pathetic sound.

Where is the word positioned in the sentence? Placing a word at the beginning or the end of a sentence can emphasise it. Repeating a word can add even more emphasis.
e.g. Dead – she could not believe he was dead!

Here the repetition of the word and the fact that it is placed at the beginning and the end of the sentence help to stress the significance of the word and the character's shock.

How is the word presented? Has a different font or text size been used? Has it been made bold, italic, underlined, coloured or highlighted? All of these things can make a particular word stand out and can affect how the word is read.
e.g. 'It was *so* unfair!'

If this sentence was spoken, the 'so' would be stressed because it is in italics. This type of emphasis gives the impression that the phrase is being uttered by a child.

Analysing Sentences

The most obvious thing to look for is the length of sentences. Short sentences can be used to speed up the reader for a specific reason, for example, for a dramatic effect or to show panic. Long sentences can be used to build up a picture in the reader's mind, to follow a train of thought or to prolong the tension. You should then look at what type of sentence it is. It could be…

- a statement
- a command
- a question (or rhetorical question)
- an exclamation.

Statements (declaratives) are sentences that state fact. These are found in all kinds of texts and do not usually need to be commented upon.
e.g. You are reading this page.

Commands (imperatives) can show that a character is in control or in a position of power or authority. Just think about how many commands your teachers and parents give you each day!
e.g. 'Sit down and shut up'.

Questions (interrogatives) can show that the writer or character is questioning something or that they are confused.
e.g. 'What do you mean?'

Rhetorical questions are questions that do not expect an answer and can be used to make the reader think about a certain point.
e.g. Is it fair that children are starving?

Exclamations can indicate how a character is feeling and show strong emotions such as anger, shock, surprise, happiness, indignation, etc.
e.g. 'You cannot do that!'

Sentences can be divided into different parts called **clauses** and **phrases**. A clause has to have a subject and a verb; it is a complete grammatical unit. A phrase is a fragment of a sentence which does not necessarily need a verb in it.

Clause

The doctor, who looked tired and worried , had just returned from America.

The beautiful girl walked carefully down the catwalk

Phrase

Sentences or phrases can be repeated in order to stress them to the reader. Remember that repetition is usually used to reinforce an idea.
e.g. Is it fair that people in the developing world are starving? Is it fair that they do not have proper medicines? Is it fair that children are suffering?

The reader is being asked to think about the fairness of the situation by the repetition of the phrase (and the rhetorical question) – 'Is it fair…?'

Analysing the Whole Text

At this level you are expected to write about the text as a whole, paying particular attention to…

- content, i.e. what it is about
- audience (see p.14)
- tone
- mood and atmosphere
- purpose (see p.15)
- style (see p.12)
- themes
- structure and presentation (see p.9).

You might be asked to summarise parts of the text. This means rewriting it in your own words, focusing on the main points. Read the text below.

> The main cause for students' disaffection at secondary school is that lessons in classrooms are not as fast and exciting as the television programmes that they watch at night. In Big Brother, the contestants use very colourful language and talk about a range of subjects and the action changes every few seconds.

You might be asked to write in your own words the main reason why the writer thinks that children in secondary school become disaffected. You could write:
e.g. According to the writer, students become bored because they do not find lessons as interesting as television programmes such as Big Brother.

Style

The term **style** refers to the way the author communicates to the reader. Aspects that can influence the overall style of a piece of writing include…
- the language used by the writer, and the way it is used
- the tone used
- the way sentences are constructed
- the narrative structure, e.g. past or present tense, the use of flashbacks, etc.
- the balance between action, character description and characters' thoughts.

As we can see from the previous pages, the purpose of the text can affect the style in which it is written. In the Reading Paper you will be expected to be able to write about the style that a text is written in and the effect that this has on the reader. For example, if a text has been written in, or is set in, a different period of time, this could affect the style of writing that has been used.

What to Look For

In the test you may be asked to…
- write about the writer's choice of words and what it shows
- discuss what certain words suggest
- comment on the negative (bad) and positive (good) effect of different words
- comment on the atmosphere that is created (what the place seems like to you)
- give your impressions (ideas) of the effect the writing creates
- quote from the passage to support your ideas.

Extract from *Great Expectations* by Charles Dickens

When I told the clerk that I would take a turn in the air while I waited, he advised me to go round the corner and I should come into Smithfield. So I came into Smithfield, and the shameful place, being all asmear with filth and fat and blood and foam, seemed to stick to me. So I rubbed it off with all possible speed by turning into a street where I saw the great black dome of St. Paul's bulging at me from behind a grim stone building which a bystander said was Newgate Prison.

Reading through this extract we can pick out some features that show the style of the piece of writing:
- the text sounds very formal
- the words highlighted in orange show that the text was written many years ago as they are phrases that we do not use commonly today
- the words highlighted in blue are used to create an image of a dirty, filthy place
- the harshness of the words has a strong effect on the reader, and helps them to clearly imagine the repellent atmosphere and the disgust the narrator feels ('filth… seemed to stick to me. So I rubbed it off with all possible speed').

Genre

A **genre** is the category of writing to which a text belongs, e.g. the film X-Men belongs to the genre of science fiction films, Pirates of the Caribbean belongs to the action adventure / pirates genre, and Notting Hill belongs to the love story genre.

The typical features of some different genres are outlined below. In the test, look out for the vocabulary, places and characters in the extracts to see which genre the writing may come from.

Love Stories / Romances

- Lovely surroundings
- Lovers meeting
- Positive diction and words associated with love and romance, e.g. cuddle, kiss, hug, etc.
- Words associated with emotions (emotive diction)

Horror Stories and the Supernatural

- Creatures, ghosts
- Evil deeds
- A mad inventor
- Spooky vocabulary, e.g. dark, creepy
- Darkness and night-time
- Woods and forests
- Mansions, old houses and castles

Cowboy Stories

- Old-fashioned towns
- Cowboys and Indians
- Battles
- Horses
- Cow herding
- A hero
- A villain

Myths and Legends

- Set in the past
- Strange creatures, like Medusa, the woman with snakes for hair
- Soldiers and heroes
- Unusual vocabulary
- Battles
- Vikings

Action and Adventure and Real Life Adventures

- An explorer, the hero
- Strange places and locations, like a jungle or a foreign country
- 'Bad' guys
- Fighting and trickery
- Treasure, maps and discoveries
- Harsh conditions

Pirate Stories

- Sea battles
- Adventures
- Treasure
- Good and bad pirates
- Galleons and ships
- Beaches and jungles

Science Fiction and Space Adventures

- Space and different planets
- Set in the future
- Robots and inventors
- Spaceships and spacemen or aliens
- Unusual and sometimes made-up vocabulary
- Strange inventions

Time Travel / Futuristic

- New inventions
- Lands that have changed
- Unusual places
- Strange creatures
- New and made-up vocabulary
- Existing in different time zones

Audience

The **audience** at a music concert is easy to describe. It is the people that are watching and listening to the concert. They go to the concert because they like the music. Obviously different bands attract different audiences. You and your parents would probably not go to see the same band!

However, the audience for a text is different. Different people can read the text and, as with a band or singer, some people will be interested in what they read and others will not.

Some texts are aimed at a wide audience, e.g. newspapers, charity and promotional leaflets. Others are aimed at a specialist audience, e.g. Fisherman's Weekly. The people that write the magazine will provide information that is interesting to people who like fishing and may use words and terms that are particular to that sport. You could still read it but it probably would not appeal to you or interest you if you do not like fishing.

You should try to pinpoint the audience that the text is written for, i.e. identify who the writer intended it for.

What to Look For

When looking at the texts you get in the test try to work out who it could be aimed at, e.g. a wide, general audience or a specific audience such as young children, specific hobby enthusiasts... the list is endless. The style of writing used will differ according to the audience at which it is aimed. Here are some questions to ask yourself to help you work out who the intended audience is.

- For whom is the language appropriate? Do you understand it, or is it too complicated or too simple for you? This will help you think about the age of the person it is aimed at.
- What style of language is used? Are metaphors or similes used, and if so, what? For example, text aimed at men might use sports-related metaphors.
- Does it use presentational devices, such as pictures, diagrams, graphs, etc.? Graphs or charts could be used in business reports, pictures could be used in children's books, etc.
- How is the information laid out on the page? Is it mainly text, or a mix of text and pictures? Is there a main body of text or lots of short sections?
- Are a range of fonts, colours and sizes used? Large fonts could be used for people who can't read very well (usually very young and very old people) or to highlight specific words or sections. Different fonts and colours could be used to make the text look exciting, which could mean it is aimed at teenagers.

Purpose

The **purpose** of the text is the reason that it has been written. There are three main purposes:

- **to entertain**, for example, short stories, play scripts, television scripts, poems
- **to persuade**, for example, charity leaflets, posters, advertisements, reviews
- **to inform / instruct**, for example, text books, web sites, instruction manuals.

The purpose of the writing will affect what style features, structure and presentation aides are used. Features that can be found in writing to entertain can be found on p.16–21 and features of writing to persuade and to inform / instruct are on p.22–23. If you can identify the features of different types of writing you will be able to find out its purpose.

Writing to Entertain

The main purpose of this type of writing is to occupy you. It is usually found in novels, short stories, poetry, plays, etc. Descriptive sentences are used to create images in the reader's mind. This is an extract from a short story which was written to **entertain**.

> As the great shark circled the helpless couple, they clung together, convinced that united they could defeat this enemy of the deep. The shark appeared to be watching them with its cold, inhumane eyes. Suddenly, Jon felt a tugging on his leg; he knew that the battle had commenced. He would do anything he could to save Sophie, even if it cost him his life.

Writing to Persuade

The main purpose of writing to persuade is to convince the reader that the writer's opinion is correct. You might find this type of writing in a newspaper or magazine article, in a charity leaflet, etc. This text is trying to **persuade** you that sharks are not cruel killers.

> The great white shark is a magnificent creature and it has been given some bad press in recent years. It is not the great killer of the deep that many would have us believe. In fact, researchers have proved that these superb creatures only ever attack humans when they mistake them for seals.

Writing to Inform / Instruct

The main purpose of this type of writing is to give you information about a topic or tell you how to do something. It is usually found in instruction manuals, on leaflets, internet sites, etc. The text below gives **information** about a study of the great white shark.

> An interesting study conducted at the South Pacific Islands sought to find out whether a shark is visually attracted to certain prey items based solely on their shape. In this study, researchers attached several decoys to a fishing line and placed them into the water to see if the sharks would attack them.

Whereas this text gives divers **instructions** about what to do in the case of an attack.

> There are three things to remember if you are attacked by a great white shark:
> - thrashing attracts the creatures
> - aim to punch the creature on the nose or near the eyes
> - try to remain below the water.

Key Terms

Throughout your English lessons you will have looked at different types of texts and you will have learned what to look for and the terms for techniques that writers use in their work. Here is a reminder of the main terms and what effect using each of them might produce.

Tone – the attitude throughout the text, e.g. the author / narrator / character could be playful, angry, suspicious, ironic, etc. *Used to allow emotions to be expressed*.

Adverbs – describe the verb and usually end with '-ly', e.g. carefully, cautiously, quietly. *Used to add more detail to an action*.

Adjectives – describe nouns, e.g. great, harsh, unbelievable. *Used to add more detail to a noun*.

Repetition – when words, phrases, sentences or structures are repeated. *Used to stress certain words or key points*.

Alliteration – the same initial sound repeated in a string of words, e.g. big balls bounced. *Used to stress certain words and create rhythm*.

Onomatopoeia – a word that sounds like the thing it describes, e.g. splash. *Used to appeal to the reader's senses: usually hearing or sight*.

Oxymoron – contradictory words, e.g. cruel kindness. *Used to make the reader think*.

Assonance – repetition of an internal vowel sound, e.g. pull and push, or the use of the same consonant sounds, e.g. filled, fold, fooled. *Used to emphasise certain words and slow the reader's pace*.

Image – a picture created in your mind by words. *Used to involve the reader in the moment being described*.

Personification – making an object or an animal sound like a person, giving it human qualities, e.g. the fingers of the tree grabbed at my hair as I passed. *Used to enable the reader to identify with an object or an animal and helps to create a specific image*.

Simile – a comparison of one thing with another that includes the words 'as' or 'like', e.g. the man was as cold as ice. *Used to give additional information; used to create a particular effect*.

Metaphor – a vivid image created by the direct comparison of two things, e.g. the army of ants was on the rampage. Here the ants *are* an army, they are not

like an army (which would be a simile). *Used to give additional information; used to create a particular effect*.

Symbolism – a symbol is an object used to represent an abstract idea, e.g. a dove symbolises peace, red symbolises danger. *Used to suggest an idea indirectly*.

Rhyme – the patterns of the rhyming structure, e.g. regular (abab, abba) or irregular (no fixed rhyme). *Used to help set the pace of the poem*.

Rhythm – the beat of the poem, like the rhythm of a song. It can be fast or slow, strict or varied. *Used to add to the overall effect*.

Questions (interrogatives) – they can show that the writer wants the reader to consider the question, or that they themselves are wondering about the question asked. *Used to show a range of things about the character that uses them, e.g. inquisitiveness or confusion*.

Rhetorical questions – ones that do not need an answer, e.g. when your teacher asks you 'do you think that is funny?' they do not expect you to answer, they just want you to think about it! *Used to make the reader or another character think about the question that has been asked*.

Exclamations – can denote a command or show emotion, e.g. 'I hate you'. *Used to portray emotions*.

Dialect and Accent

Standard English – the conventional use of words and grammar (think of the words and sentence constructions newsreaders use). It is used in most written texts.

Dialect – the words and grammar that speakers use. Dialects differ from Standard English. Each dialect has its own special words and way of using grammar, e.g. Americans would say 'sidewalk' instead of 'pavement' and 'I got off of the bus' instead of 'I got off the bus'. *Used to show which social group, region or country a character belongs to. A writer might give two characters different types of language to use to show that they are from different social groups in order to create an immediate contrast*.

Accent – the way people sound when they speak. Accent can be conveyed through the use of non-standard spelling, e.g. 'ah wunder'd where tha'd bin' to convey a Yorkshire accent. *Used to show where the character is from*.

Play Scripts

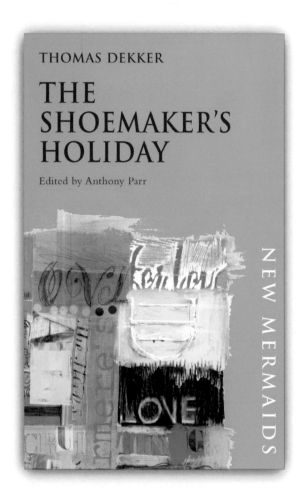

THOMAS DEKKER

THE SHOEMAKER'S HOLIDAY

Edited by Anthony Parr

NEW MERMAIDS

In this paper it is possible to get an extract from a play. Plays are meant to be performed so they are laid out to make it clear who is speaking, who is on stage, when characters make entrances and exits, etc. They will be set out in a format similar to the Shakespeare play that you have been studying. There is an extract from a play on the following page with key features pointed out. It is worthwhile bearing in mind the terms you have used when you studied your Shakespeare play. Remember that plays are written to be performed.

What to Look For

As with any text you get, you need to think about...
- content
- themes
- style.

Look out for techniques explained on the Key Terms pages (p.16) because most of them can be found in a play script. There are some other features that are specific to play scripts that you should look out for as well.

Stage Directions

These tell performers / actors how to deliver their lines. They are usually in italics. They can be found at the beginning of a scene and give information about...
- the setting – so the production crew know how to set the stage, what scenery should be in the background, what props and costumes are needed, etc.
- which characters are involved – so actors know who is in each scene
- what action the characters are involved in – e.g. sitting in a drawing room, fighting in a battle etc.

Stage directions can also be found throughout the scene to give information about...

... when characters enter and exit

> [*Exuent*]

... the tone of voice used

> **ROSE**
> [*Suspiciously*] What have you done?

... the type of speech

> **CLOWN**
> [*Aside*] Watch me play a merry joke.

... what action the character should be doing

> **ROSE**
> [*Pacing left to right across the stage*]
> How have I got myself into this mess?

Italics can also be used in speeches so the actors know which words they should emphasise, e.g. I am *so* upset, I can hardly speak.

Stage directions are suggestions for how the play can be performed, but remember, different actors and directors may interpret the instructions differently.

Opposite is an extract from the play, *The Shoemaker's Holiday* by Thomas Dekker. The notes point out the main features of the format.

Tells us which characters are entering the scene

Tells us about the action

Enter HODGE, LACY, RALPH, FIRK *and other Shoemakers in a morris. After a little dancing,* the Lord Mayor speaks

OATLEY

Master Eyre, are all these shoemakers?

EYRE

All cordwainers, my good Lord Mayor.

Said out loud to let the audience in on the characters thoughts

ROSE

[*Aside*] How like my Lacy looks yond shoemaker!   55

LACY

[*Aside*] O, that I durst but speak unto my love!

instructions given to another actor in speech. Separate stage directions are not needed

OATLEY

Sybil, go fetch some wine to make these drink. – You are all welcome.

ALL [THE SHOEMAKERS]

We thank your lordship.

Tells us the two groups are set apart

ROSE *takes a cup of wine and goes to* LACY

ROSE

For his sake whose fair shape thou represent'st,

Good friend, I drink to thee.   60

LACY

Ik be dancke, good frister.

MARGERY

I see, Mistress Rose, you do not want judgement. You have drunk to the properest man I keep.

FIRK

Here be some have done their parts to be as proper as he.   65

OATLEY

Well, urgent business calls me back to London.

Good fellows, first go in and taste our cheer,

And to make merry as you homeward go,

Spend these two angels in beer at Stratford Bow.

EYRE

To these two, my mad lads, Sim Eyre adds another. Then

cheerly, Firk, tickle it, Hans, and all for the honour of   70

shoemakers.

Tells us who leaves

All [THE SHOEMAKERS] *go dancing out*

OATLEY

Come, Master Eyre, let's have your company.

Tells us who leaves

Exuent [OATLEY, EYRE *and* MARGERY]

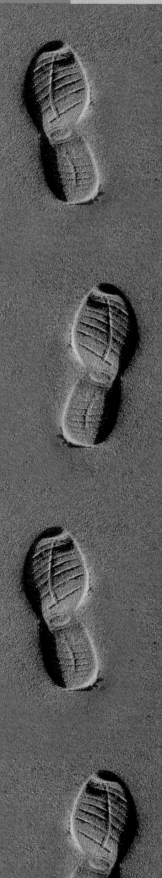

19

Prose

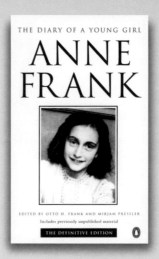

In the test you are likely to get a piece of **prose** to write about. It could be made up (fiction) or true (non-fiction). The extracts could come from different types of writing including...

- a novel or a short story
- an imaginary or real life diary
- a biography or an autobiography.

What to Look For

As well as looking for content, setting, themes and style, you should also think about the following:

Type of writing – fiction or non-fiction; literary or non-literary.

Audience and purpose – who the text is aimed at and why it has been written. The language and format will give you clues (see p.14–15).

Narrative viewpoint – the writer's opinion of the subject. This will be revealed through the words they use and the way they use them (see p.12). Look for clues that reveal what the writer is thinking. This will often be revealed through how they write about the subject.

Tone – the attitude of the passage. Does it change throughout the passage?

Structure of the passage (see p.9) – what is at the beginning, middle and end? Are there any links or logical developments, e.g. moving from positive words (sunny, bright, clear) to negative words (dark, foreboding, spooky) to show that the scene, character, mood or tone has changed.

Tenses used in the passage:
- the past (e.g. he walked) – to show what happened in the past
- the present (e.g. he walks) and present participle (e.g. walking) – to show that the action is happening now and perhaps to involve the reader in the action
- the future (e.g. he will walk) – to show a prediction of what might happen as a consequence of things that might have happened in the past. For example:

In the future

He will walk the plank due to the fact that he killed a fellow sailor.

In the past

First-person accounts –use 'I' to show the main character's or narrator's own point of view, and reveal the character's true thoughts, feelings and emotions. It can be used in a diary, an autobiography or a novel, e.g. someone might write: 'I want to get a level 6 in my English test. I've got my fingers crossed'.

Second-person accounts – use 'you' to address the reader directly. Often used in diary extracts, letters, etc.

Third-person accounts – use the pronouns 'he', 'she' and 'they' to refer to the main character. It is used when a writer is writing about others. They can tell the reader things about events thorough their own eyes rather than those of the character. For example: 'Jasmin was so pretty. Everyone loved her'. This may not be what everyone else thinks, but it is what the writer believes.

Poetry

Poems can be written about anything. There are war poems (like the one on this page), love poems, protest poems (that protest about an issue in society) and poems that describe things, places and emotions. Poems tend to be very descriptive as they use words economically to create images in the reader's mind.

Poetry is easy to spot because it is usually presented differently from prose. It is often written in stanzas (verses). Poets and literary writers frequently use the same techniques in their writing even though they may use them in different ways (their style).

What to Look For

As with all texts you should look at the content, themes and style of the piece of writing. But with poetry you should also look for the use of...
- adjectives, verbs and adverbs
- sentence types and length
- rhyme (the sound patterns)
- rhythm (the beat of the poem)
- tone
- repetition
- alliteration
- personification
- onomatopoeia.

Refer back to the Key Terms pages (p.16) if you cannot remember what every term means.

Extract from *Strange Meeting* by Wilfred Owen

It seemed that out of battle I escaped
Down some profound dull tunnel, long since scooped
Through granites which titanic wars had groined.

Yet also there encumbered sleepers groaned
Too fast in thought or death to be bestirred
Then, as I probed them, one sprang up, and stared
With piteous recognition in fixed eyes
Lifting distressful hands, as if to bless.

first-person pronoun	
tunnel is very old	
great battles	
verb shows pain / discomfort	
old-fashioned word for woken up	
adjective makes reader feel sorry for the sleepers	
adjective conveys suffering	

Non-fiction

A non-fiction text is used here to mean texts other than those covered on the previous pages. Look back at p.7 to make sure you are clear about the distinctions between fiction / non-fiction and literary / non-literary.

These are some examples of non-fiction texts:
- newspaper / magazine articles
- extracts from text books
- diary entries written by a real person
- instruction booklets and manuals
- web pages about a certain topic
- fact sheets
- information leaflets aimed at certain audiences, e.g. school prospectuses.

Whereas the main purpose of fiction texts is to entertain the audience, the main purpose of non-fiction texts is quite different and can be divided into two categories:
- writing to inform / instruct (to give you facts)
- writing to persuade (as used in advertising, by charity leaflets, etc.).

Remember that a text can have more than one purpose and cannot always be placed easily into one of the two categories; writing that instructs and gives you information can also be persuasive. You need to look for its primary purpose (see p.15).

What to Look For in Informative / Instructional Writing

Features of writing to inform / instruct include…
- headings and subheadings that divide up the text
- information presented clearly
- simple and direct sentences being used to get information across
- words that are more factual than emotive
- stories being used to get facts across, e.g. a factual story about an explorer's journey
- images or charts to help present information.

Look at the piece of writing below.

> Roxy, a champion thoroughbred racehorse, won the 3.15pm race at Doncaster today by 4 lengths.

This text just states the facts about a horse winning a race, so it informs.

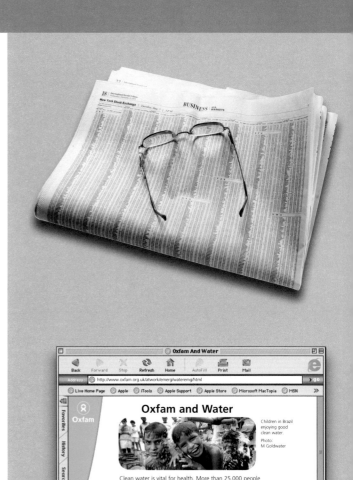

What to Look For in Persuasive Writing

Writing to persuade uses many of the features of fiction writing to create a particular effect or evoke a particular emotional response in the reader (see p.15). Always think about content, audience, purpose and style (what is being said, who it's being aimed at, why, and how it is written) whatever text you are reading. Here are some other features to look for...

Images or pictures appeal to your emotions, e.g. a dying seal pup in an anti-seal culling (killing) campaign leaflet could have a much stronger effect on someone than the words in the article.

Graphs, **diagrams**, etc. together with their subheadings can give information or illustrate a point that is made in the text.

Formatting, such as bold, italics or larger font size can be used to stress certain words.

Colours can be used to appeal to the reader, e.g. red to stress danger.

Emotive words are words that appeal to your emotions to make you react in a certain way, e.g. a campaign for a children's charity could include a sentence like: 'The small, defenceless child was subjected to unimaginable cruelty'. This sentence contains strong, descriptive words that appeal to your emotions and make you feel pity for the child, which means you are more likely to want to help her. Also, focusing on one child personalises the request for help; the reader feels the urge to help that particular child. If the leaflet said 'There's 30,000 starving children' the reader might easily think 'well what difference can I make?'.

Choice of **adjectives**, **verbs** and **adverbs** can have a great impact on the effect of the text on the reader (as in the example above), e.g. 'the seal pup was killed' sounds bad, but 'the seal pup was slaughtered' sounds much worse.

Rhetorical questions can be used very effectively in this style of writing.

Exclamations can be used to stress a certain sentence.

Structure of the text – the way it begins, what is in the middle and how it ends – is very important. The text must have a logical flow otherwise the reader will not be able to follow the point that is being made.

The text below gives you the facts about a case of animal cruelty that has been investigated by a charity but it also uses emotive language. This results in a very persuasive piece of writing which has the primary purpose of trying to persuade the audience to donate some money to help Bentley and other animals like him.

> When he was rescued, Bentley was a skeletal dog, who cowered every time any men approached him. He hated being in the dark, probably because he had been kept in a cold, dark shed, and he ate his food quickly whenever it was provided. He was petrified of drinking water from his dish, preferring instead to lick the dampness off the floor, because attempts had been made to drown him.

Approaching Test Questions

Now that we have covered all the skills necessary to do well in the test, it is time to look at how to tackle the test paper.

In the test you will be given 15 minutes to read through the booklet that contains all the extracts. During this time it is a good idea to underline phrases that you might be able to use as quotes and make notes in the margin, perhaps writing short phrases to sum up what each section is about. You will find this very useful when you come to write your answers as it means you will be more familiar with the text, and it should help you to find the relevant bit of the text more easily.

Annotating the Extracts

- Underline emotive words.
- Underline and label any literary techniques used, e.g. metaphor, repetition, etc.
- Write brief phrases about what happens in each paragraph to remind yourself when you come to answer the questions.
- Note any special features of the writing, e.g. use of headings, pictures, charts, etc.

What to Do in the Test

- Read the question carefully then re-read the relevant part of the passage and highlight words that are relevant to the question.
- Look at the space provided to work out roughly how long your answer should be.
- Look at how many marks are awarded and try to make that many points.
- Back up every point you make with a quote and explain it (PEE).

Test Questions

In the Reading Paper there are some questions that require shorter answers and some that require longer answers.

The shorter questions are easier to answer because they only require brief responses. However, make sure you read the question carefully and answer the question that is being asked. If you are asked to write bullet points or to fill in a table, make sure you keep your responses brief and to the point.

The longer questions are worth five marks, so try to make at least five good points (using PEE). Again, you must answer the question that is being asked so read it carefully.

There are many different methods of planning you can use including…
- making lists
- drawing spider diagrams
- using symbols to organise your thoughts.

You can find examples of these in the Shakespeare section of this book. Experiment with different methods for planning to see which one works best for you. Whichever method you decide to use, make sure you use the PEE technique. This will make sure you back up everything you say with a quote and will mean that you should be able to structure your answer and mention all the relevant points. This is especially important in the longer questions.

Below is an extract, a text-style question and advice on how you could tackle answering the question in the test.

Extract from *Treasure Island* by Robert Louis Stevenson.

Shaken as I was with these alarms it was hard for me to keep up with the rapid pace of the treasure-hunters. Now and again I stumbled; and it was then that Silver plucked so roughly at the rope and launched at me his murderous glances.

We were now on the margin of the thicket.

'Hurry, mate, all together!' shouted Merry: and the foremost of us broke into a run.

And suddenly, not ten yards further, we beheld them stop. A low cry arose. Silver doubled his pace, digging away with the foot of his crutch like one possessed: and the next moment he and I had come to a complete halt.

Before us was a great excavation, not very recent, for the sides had fallen in and grass had sprouted at the bottom. In this were the shaft of a pick broken in two and the boards of several packing-cases strewn around. On one of theses boards I saw, branded with a hot iron, the name Walrus – the name of Flint's ship.

All was clear. The cache [hidden treasure] had been found and rifled; the seven hundred thousand pounds were gone!

Test-style Question

In the last section of the text how is the reader prepared for the discovery that the treasure has gone? You should comment on…
- how the men's approach is described
- the gradual revelation that something is wrong
- the way the text ends.

Planning Your Answer

Firstly, it will help you to focus on the question if you underline the key words. Then you can start planning your answer. Using the list approach, here is one way you could plan your answer. It takes each aspect that you are asked to comment on and finds a quote from the extract to illustrate each point.

Describe men's approach…
- stumbling, running fast, 'rapid pace' – makes reader read fast, creates speed and excitement, indicates coming to a climax
- 'suddenly' they all stop – unexpected, shows something has gone wrong
- simile – 'digging away… like one possessed', suggests frantic movement

Gradual realisation something is wrong…
- 2 paragraphs given to lead up to treasure being gone – description delays moment of discovery, builds reader up to the realisation – 'a great excavation, not very recent'

End of text…
- states facts 'the seven hundred thousand pounds were gone!', ends with exclamation to show the shock they feel.

The following pages have an annotated extract followed by test-style questions and model answers so you can prepare yourself for the different types of extracts and questions you might get in the Reading test.

Extract from a Novel (I)

Extract from *Wuthering Heights* by Emily Brontë

It was a very dark evening for summer. The clouds appeared inclined to thunder, and I said we had all better sit down: the approaching rain would be certain to bring him home without further trouble. However, Catherine would not be persuaded into tranquillity. She kept wandering to and fro, from the gate to the door, in a state of agitation which permitted no response, and at length took up a permanent situation on one side of the wall, near the road, where, heedless of my expostulations and the growling thunder, and the great drops that began to plash around her, she remained, calling at intervals, and then listening, and then crying outright. She beat Hareton, or any child, at a good passionate fit of crying.

About midnight, while we still sat up, the storm came rattling over the Heights in full fury. There was a violent wind, as well as thunder, and either one or the other split a tree off at the corner of the building: a huge bow fell across the roof, and knocked down a portion of the east chimney stack, sending a clatter of stones and soot into the kitchen fire. We thought a bolt had fallen in the middle of us, and Joseph swung on his knees, beseeching the Lord to remember the patriarchs Noah and Lot.

But the uproar passed away in twenty minutes, leaving us all unharmed, excepting Cathy, who got thoroughly drenched for her obstinacy in refusing to take shelter, and standing bonnetless and shawl-less to catch as much water as she could with her hair and clothes. She came in and lay down on the settle, all soaked as she was, turning her face to the back and putting her hands before it.

Sets the scene. Dark, looks like a storm is coming. Weather reflects Catherine's mood. She's unsettled and upset about something.

Catherine is very upset.

Joseph starts to pray.

Turns away from the group. Doesn't want to talk to them.

Thunder storm starts.

Later on that evening. Storm still raging, causing damage.

Everyone is fine except for Cathy. She's stubbornly stayed outside and got wet.

1. In paragraph 1, the phrase 'Catherine would not be persuaded into tranquillity' (a state of being calm) suggests that Cathy is very upset. Identify two other words or phrases from paragraph 1 which also suggest this.

   a) she kept wandering to and fro... in a state of agitation

   b) crying outright

   (1 mark)

2. In paragraph 2 the storm is described as hitting the house in 'full fury'. What does this suggest about the storm?

   The phrase 'full fury' suggests that the storm is violent and angry. The alliteration of the 'f' sound helps the words to sound forceful.

   (1 mark)

3. Paragraph 4 ends with the sentence: 'She came in and lay down on the settle, all soaked as she was, turning her face to the wall and putting her hands before it'. This suggests that Catherine is very upset. Explain how the rest of the passage creates this impression. Use quotations to prove the points that you make.

   Throughout the passage we get the impression that Catherine is very upset. The storm seems to reflect her mood. She, like the storm, is agitated and full of 'fury'. She keeps pacing to and fro in a 'state of agitation', which shows that she is unsettled.

   Even though she is getting wet through, and the narrator keeps asking her to come into the house, she will not and keeps calling out. It seems that she is worried about the person who is out in the storm. She is crying as much as a child would. When the full storm hits, Cathy does not take shelter, instead she stands out in the storm without her bonnet or shawl on meaning that she gets wet through. She is 'thoroughly drenched for her obstinacy' which means she gets soaked because she stubbornly refuses to take shelter.

   At the end of the extract she comes in to the house and turns her face to the wall which shows she does not wish to talk to anyone.

   (3 marks)

1

These are examples of shorter test-style questions. Look at the model answers, but remember there is not only one correct answer.

- The answers use the space provided.
- In question 3, the answer summarises the extract. This means the pupil has explained what is happening in their own words.
- Each answer uses quotes from the extract to illustrate the points being made.

Other things you might be asked to comment on when discussing an extract from a novel are...

- sentence structures and particular phrases
- the use of punctuation
- particular adjectives and adverbs used for effect
- the overall impact of the passage
- the structure of the passage – what happens in the beginning, the middle and the end?
- the writer's point of view.

Extract from a Novel (II)

Extract from *A Christmas Carol* by Charles Dickens

When Scrooge awoke, it was so dark, that looking out of bed, he could scarcely distinguish the transparent window from the opaque walls of his chamber. He was endeavouring to pierce the darkness with his ferret eyes, when the chimes of a neighbouring church struck the four quarters. So he listened for the hour.

To his great astonishment the heavy bell went on from six to seven, and from seven to eight, and regularly up to twelve; then stopped. Twelve. It was past two when he went to bed. The clock was wrong. An icicle must have got into the works. Twelve.

He touched the spring of his repeater, to correct this most preposterous clock. Its rapid little pulse beat twelve: and stopped.

'Why, it isn't possible,' said Scrooge, 'that I can have slept through a whole day and far into another night. It isn't possible that anything has happened to the sun, and this is twelve at noon.'

The idea being an alarming one, he scrambled out of bed, and groped his way to the window. He was obliged to rub the frost off with the sleeve of his dressing-gown before he could see anything; and could see very little then. All he could make out was, that it was still very foggy and extremely cold, and that there was no noise of people running to and fro, and making a great stir, as there unquestionably would have been if night had beaten off bright day, and taken possession of the world. This was a great relief, because 'Three days after sight of this First of Exchange pay to Mr. Ebenezer Scrooge on his order,' and so forth, would have become a mere United States security if there were no days to count by.

Scrooge went to bed again, and thought, and thought, and thought it over and over, and could make nothing of it. The more he thought, the more perplexed he was; and, the more he endeavoured not to think, the more he thought.

Marley's Ghost bothered him exceedingly. Every time he resolved within himself, after mature inquiry that it was all a dream, his mind flew back again, like a strong spring released, to its first position, and presented the same problem to be worked all through, 'Was it a dream or not?'

It's so dark he can't see

Shocked when he hears the time

Vivid descriptions: 'very', 'extreme'

Shows his priorities by worrying about the impact a lack of days and nights would have on his money

Can't work out what is happening

Confused

1. How does the writer's use of language in this extract suggest that the character Scrooge is confused and finds himself in an unusual situation?

The writer's use of language suggests that the character is confused and finds himself in an unusual situation. Firstly, he cannot really tell the difference between the walls of his bedroom and the window which tells us that it is very dark and this could make him confused. **◄ 1**

Then the writer tells us, 'To his great astonishment,' the bells outside continued to chime. It seems that time has gone backwards because the clock stopped at twelve but he did not go to bed until two o'clock. The word, 'twelve' is repeated which shows his confusion. He thinks that this is strange and decides that an icicle must have got in the clock, which would be an unusual situation. He thinks that the clock is 'preposterous', meaning stupid. This shows he is confused about what is going on. He says to himself that 'it isn't possible'. This shows that the situation is very unusual. **◄ 2**

We are told that he 'scrambled out of bed.' The verb 'scrambled' shows that he is not very calm and finds his situation strange. **◄ 3**

We are told that the more he thinks the more confused he becomes. He 'thought and thought and thought'. The repetition of the word shows he is trying to make sense of what is happening. His mind is like a 'strong spring' bouncing all over the place. The simile shows his confusion further, comparing his mind to something that is all over the place like a spring. **◄ 4**

The final sentence is a question; the question he is asking himself, 'Was it a dream or not?' This shows how strange he finds the whole situation. He wonders whether he is having a dream or if the situation is real. **◄ 5**

(5 marks)

1

Below is a commentary on the model answer to a longer-style question.

1 The first sentence explains the focus of the question. and summarises what happens in the first part of the extract. Quotes are used to make the first point.

2 Second point focuses on Scrooge's confusion. Explains what is happening to make Scrooge confused, and the conclusions that Scrooge comes to. Examples are provided.

3 Again, describes the action and explains what this could mean.

4 Quotes are used to focus on the text and terminology is used correctly – verb, repetition, simile – and explains why they are used, what effect they create.

5 Identifies the question at the end of the extract. Explains the significance of Scrooge asking himself this question.

Extract from a Newspaper Article

- alliteration used to increase force of words

- this paragraph gives the facts
- 'flash' used to show how quickly it happened
- negative sensational words used

- this paragraph concentrates on how one man was affected
- language (e.g. victim) used to make you feel sorry for him
- quote used

- in this paragraph the tone changes from sad to happy/uplifting
- all in same position but no point wallowing in it, celebrate instead
- quote from another villager used

thenews

Flash Floods Devastate Local Villages

Flash floods devastated many villages in Derbyshire overnight on Friday 4 November 2005. The full extent of the destruction is not yet known, but one thing is for certain, repairing the damaged property and getting people's lives back to normal could take months, if not years.

Charlie's submerged fish and chip shop

Sand bags holding back the flood waters

Destruction

One victim of the floods was Charlie Turner, 54, from Leafdale. He awoke on Saturday morning to find his home and garden swamped under a metre of water. But there was more bad news waiting for him in the nearby town of Greenham when he went to open up his family business, Charlie's Chippie. He found flood water halfway up the walls and his deep-fat fryers completely submerged, so there's no chance of a fish supper until the water abates. Says Charlie, 'This chippie has been open six days a week since my grandfather opened it in 1960. I feel like I'm letting down the family name by closing up'.

Celebration

Every villager in Leafdale has a similar story to tell, but this community can't be brought down that easily. Even though the communal bonfire they had all helped to build the previous week had been washed across the park, they decided to go ahead and celebrate Bonfire Night anyway. They all met in the park, bringing with them whatever fireworks they had that hadn't been wrecked in the flood, and managed to produce an impressive display. 'It'll take more than a bit of water to dampen our spirits' joked local farmer, Jack Marchmont, 57.

1. What does the choice of language in paragraphs 1 and 2 tell us about how the flood has affected Charlie?

We are told that his house and garden have been flooded, so it has affected his family life.

The deep fat fryers in his chippie are described as being 'completely submerged' which means his working life will be badly disrupted.

He feels he is 'letting down the family name' by not being able to open his chippie, which would make him feel bad.

(3 marks)

2. Complete the table below to show how the language used in the paragraph about the village as a community contrasts with the language used to describe the effect the flood has had on Charlie Turner's life.

	Language used
Charlie Turner	*focuses on the bad aspects:* *'damage', 'destruction', 'bad news'*
Village	*Focuses on getting over it:* *'can't be brought down that easily'*

(2 marks)

1

Again, look at how the responses answer the questions that have been asked:

- The answers use the space provided.
- Question 1 is worth three marks, so three points have been made.
- In question 2 a table is provided, and the candidate has provided answers of an appropriate length.
- Each answer uses quotes from the extract to illustrate the points being made.

Aspects you may be asked to comment on in a newspaper article include...

- headlines
- pictures
- emotive language
- facts
- structure – the beginning / middle / end
- particular words and phrases.

Extract from a Diary Entry

Extract from *Diary of a Storm Chaser* by Kirby Dangerfield

Sets us up for what he'll be writing about. Explains how important storm chasing is to him.

It was the week leading up to Sunday 4th December – it should have been a good week for storms and I was excited at the prospect of chasing the storm. This was more than my hobby; it was my life. I had been discussing the prospects of the storm with some colleagues. The conditions were looking healthy. There was a trough of low pressure and stiff winds on the coast should supply moisture, although Northwesterly winds dominated above 850mb, the dew points would still be reasonable. The bad news was that middle-layer moisture would be in abundance which might mean I wouldn't be able to see the storm if it did happen. I tried not to become disheartened as this would not achieve anything.

Technical language used to explain conditions. Throughout article says how he is feeling.

Eyeball analysis just means 'observation'. Again, talks about the conditions.

On Sunday morning when I did my eyeball analysis I was not overly impressed by what I saw. The sky was dominated by low cloud from the North. The temperature wasn't as warm as I'd hoped either - only around 19°C. These were not good signs: they suggested that the storm would pass rather than wreak havoc.

The first showers in the storm area started at about 10.30am. As I set off for the infamous Orange Pass I could feel my excitement building. There was nothing quite like the build up to an impressive storm. However, conditions at the top of the pass were not ideal for storm chasing. Low cloud hung like a tablecloth along the escarpment. Visibility was unbelievably poor. I felt a blanket of despair enveloping me.

Feels excited but then mood changes. Landmark, sounds notorious. Simile and metaphor used.

Mood changes. Excited because he thinks he'll see the storm, but is soon disappointed.

This didn't last for long though. When I tuned in the radio the lightning static was a constant, impressively loud noise. My mood immediately received a jolt back to positive, excitement building up again. I pushed on further, my anticipation building. But, to my dismay, although the fog lifted the cloud did not. At Dubbo I finally saw clouds ahead. However, my excitement was to come to nothing - the storm had no structure visible. All I saw was a short sharp shower of heavy rain and a few hailstones before the sun came out. Sunshine usually makes people happy, but it had the opposite effect on me as it meant that there would be no storm. I could not believe it.

Such is the life of the storm chaser. You can run - but the storms can hide. I made my way back disheartened and disappointed but I'd be ready for next time.

Alters a cliché to suit his purpose. Disappointed but won't stop trying.

1. What phrase in paragraph 2 explains that things are not going to plan for the narrator?

He says that he was not 'overly impressed' as the things that he was seeing were not good signs. The low cloud and the temperature suggested that the storm would pass and he did not want this to happen.

(1 mark)

2. In paragraph 3 the writer says he feels 'a blanket of despair enveloping me'. What does this suggest about how he is feeling?

The metaphor suggests that he is getting depressed by the idea that he might not see a storm; he will have had a wasted journey. The word, 'enveloping,' suggests that the feeling has overtaken him.

(1 mark)

3. Explain how the second half of paragraph 3 suggests that the conditions are not ideal for storm chasing. Find two quotations from this paragraph that support this idea.

- *'Low cloud hung like a tablecloth along the escarpment.'*
- *'Visibility was unbelievably poor.'*

(2 mark)

4. In paragraph 4 the writer is given a 'jolt back to positive'. What does this suggest about his mood before and after this?

This quote shows us that he had been feeling disappointed earlier but now he feels suddenly much better about his chances of finding a storm – it jolts him which suggests he was not expecting to feel this. It shows that he is hopeful that something might happen.

(1 mark)

1

Again, note all the information that can be taken from the question (the wording, the marks and space available to write the answer) has been used to write the answers:

- the answers use the space provided
- each answer uses quotes from the extract to illustrate the points being made.

When you are asked to comment on a diary entry you might be asked to look at the following aspects...

- the structure of the passage
- the use of images / pictures / subheadings
- the use of the first person 'I'
- the use of particular words and phrases that show what the writer is thinking and feeling
- the style (words used).

Test Tips

Now you should be fully prepared for the Reading Test. If you are unsure about any aspects of the test or what you have read, ask your teacher or one of your parents to explain them to you. Older brothers and sisters can also come in handy!

Remember to…
- read the passages carefully in your 15 minutes' planning time
- think about audience, purpose and style
- look carefully at titles – the words and how they look (font sizes and colour)
- underline key words and phrases in the passages
- read the questions carefully and underline important words
- read the passages again once you have read the questions and underline relevant aspects
- take note of how many marks the answers are worth
- answer the question set! Even if it is a sensible comment, you will not receive marks for a statement that does not answer the set question.

Key Words and What They Mean

Do not let the words in the questions put you off. Here are definitions of some words you might come across in test questions.

Positive – good.

Negative – not good.

Emphasises – made to stand out.

Quotation – a line from the text with quotation marks around it.

Choice of language – the words that the writer uses.

Suggests – makes you think of.

Overall impression or **what impression do you get** – what do you think or how does it affect you?

What atmosphere is created? – how do the words that the writer uses create the feelings or the mood in the text?

The writer's use / choice of language – comment on the words that are used and all the things you have revised in this section of your revision guide.

Summarising (writing a summary) – rewrite what the author has written briefly in your own words. You will be expected to make the main points of the text in a few sentences.

And finally, a couple of things it is easy to forget in an examination:

Paragraphs are the chunks of text divided by white spaces.

Punctuation is the marks that divide the text (covered on p.8).

The Shakespeare Paper

Important Information

About the Shakespeare Paper

- It tests your analytical skills.
- It lasts for 45 minutes.
- There are 18 marks available.

This paper is designed to test your knowledge and understanding of a play by William Shakespeare. You don't need to have read the whole play, but it will help if you have seen a live production or a video and/or been given a summary of the play.

In the test you will be given a booklet which contains two short pieces of text: one extract from each of the two sections you have studied during the year. You will be given one question to answer about these pieces.

What is Being Tested?

The question will relate to one of four possible **assessment focuses**. You need to know which of these focuses you are dealing with and how to tackle it.

- If the question mentions **language**, your focus is obviously **language**.
- If you are asked to discuss the play in more general terms, the focus is **ideas, themes and issues**.
- If the question mentions **actors, acting or directing**, you need to focus on the **text in performance**.
- If you are asked to discuss **named characters** from the play (e.g. Lady Macbeth, Claudio, Richard) and **how they behave**, but actors or directing are not mentioned, the focus is **character and motivation**.

All of these aspects are inter-linked: you cannot write about one without mentioning the others. As you revise your play, you should think about all four areas. You should re-read any notes you have made or been given in class and make new notes. All of this will be useful when you answer the test question, but make sure you keep the question's focus at the front of your mind. This way you will answer the question you have been set and not the one you hoped would be set.

About this Section of the Revision Guide

This section of the revision guide will take each of the four focuses in turn, explain what they mean and give you some ideas about how to approach them. It will also show you ways of approaching the question and planning your answer for each focus. There will be an extract from a different play by Shakespeare for each focus and part of a model answer to a question about those extracts. You will probably only be familiar with one of these plays, but by reading the extracts, notes and answers on all of them, you will learn how to go about answering a similar question on your own play. It is up to you to take the hints and advice given in each section and apply them to the play you have studied.

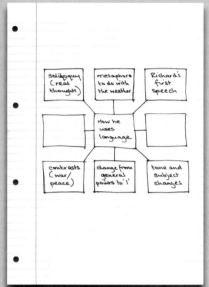

Spider Diagram

List

Paragraph Plan

Reading the Question and Annotating the Extracts

It may seem like an obvious point, but make sure you read the question properly and underline the key words in the question. Although you will know the selected scenes very well by the time you do your test it is important to remember that the extracts on which the questions are based are only part of what you have studied. As soon as you have read the question, it is a good idea to read through the extract, making notes or highlighting key points as you go. Remember, you can write on the question paper – this can be a great help.

Planning

Planning your answer is essential if you are going to stay focused on the question while you are writing. There are many different ways of planning:

- drawing a 'spider diagram'
- making lists under headings
- doing a paragraph plan
- using a grid.

You might know by now which one works best for you. If you do not, you should experiment with different ways of planning as part of your revision. Some examples of ways of planning will be covered in this guide. It's entirely up to you how you plan your answer, but do not spend too long on it – about five to ten minutes should be enough.

PEE

In your answer you need to make sure everything you say is rooted in the text. In other words, whatever you say has to be backed up by references: either direct quotations from the text or paraphrases. Before you start writing, remind yourself to use **PEE (Point, Evidence, Explanation)**:

P make your Point
E back it up with Evidence from the text
E Explain what the evidence means

Shakespeare's Language

Although **Shakespeare's language** can be difficult to understand, he often uses language to tell us about his characters and their behaviour, and about themes and ideas. Here are some of the features of language you might look out for. You should be familiar with the words in bold, but you can refer back to the Reading Paper section (p.16–17) if you need to refresh your memory.

Imagery

Characters' choice of **vocabulary** (the kind of words they use) can tell us something about how they are feeling, their motivation and their attitudes. They might use **imagery** connected to war, the weather, or love. Think about what this could tell you about the character and the themes of the play.

In *Much Ado About Nothing,* Claudio uses a **simile** to express his mistaken belief that Hero is not a virgin, comparing her both to the Roman goddess of love and to animals:

> But you are more intemperate in your blood
> Than Venus or those pamper'd animals
> That rage in savage sensuality
> (Much Ado About Nothing Act 4 Scene 1)

Richard uses **metaphors** connected with the weather to convey the sudden, huge change in the fortunes of his family, the House of York:

> Now is the winter of our discontent
> Made glorious summer by this son of York
> (Richard III Act 1 Scene 1)

The word son here is also a **pun**, because it can mean two things: taken literally it means that the king is a son of the House of York; but it also compares him to the sun as the source of the prosperity of the nation. Some characters use a lot of sexual or vulgar puns; what might this tell us about them?

A particular type of metaphor, often used by Shakespeare, is **personification**. In *Richard III,* Buckingham talks about England as if the country were a sick and disabled woman: 'The noble isle does want her proper limbs' *(Act 3 Scene 7).*

Other Techniques

Repetition may be used to emphasise a word or phrase, showing that it represents an important idea or feeling: 'Tomorrow, and tomorrow, and tomorrow' *(Macbeth Act 5 Scene 5)*.

Alliteration can create a certain tone or feeling. For example, a string of words beginning with the letter 's' can sound sinister and threatening: 'side-stitches that shall pen thy breath up' *(The Tempest Act 1 Scene 4)*. Words beginning with 'k' or 'g' can sound harsh and threatening. Think about what impression other sounds might create.

Shakespeare often uses contrast and opposition to make a point. You might come across an **oxymoron**, where two words with opposite meanings are put together, perhaps to show the speaker's confusion or the untrustworthiness of the person he speaks about, as when Claudio speaks of 'pure impiety and impious purity' *(Much Ado About Nothing Act 4 Scene 1)*.

You will sometimes find lists of connected ideas; these usually come in threes. Buckingham uses this technique when he tries to persuade Richard to accept the crown by emphasising just what Richard would be giving up if he declines:

> Know then it is your fault you that you resign
> The supreme seat, the throne majestical,
> The sceptred office of your ancestors
> (Richard III Act 3 Scene 7)

Rhetorical questions do not require an answer. Macbeth's use of them reflect his uncertainty and worry: 'What's the boy Malcolm? / Was he not born of woman?' *(Act 5 Scene 3)*.

You should also look at punctuation. **Dashes**, **colons** or **semi-colons** can show that a character's speech is hesitant or jerky, perhaps because of nervousness or excitement, like Banquo's just before his murder:

> Hold, take my sword - There's husbandry in heaven;
> Their candles are all out: - take thee that too
> (Macbeth Act 2 Scene 1)

Shakespeare's Language

Approaching the Question

Here is a question that focuses on language.

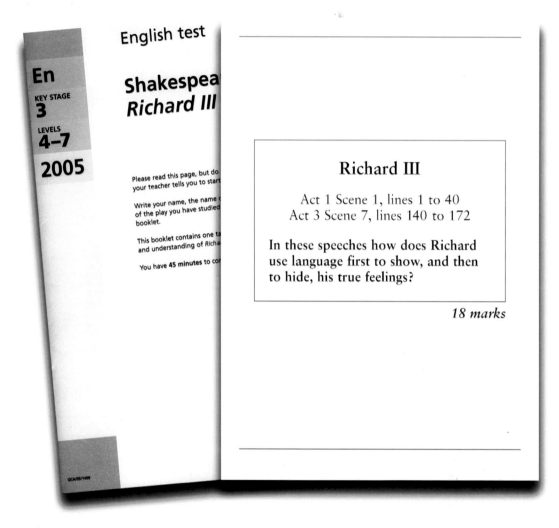

English test

En
KEY STAGE
3
LEVELS
4–7
2005

Shakespea
Richard III

Please read this page, but do
your teacher tells you to start

Write your name, the name
of the play you have studied
booklet.

This booklet contains one ta
and understanding of Richa

You have 45 minutes to co

QCA/05/1409

Richard III

Act 1 Scene 1, lines 1 to 40
Act 3 Scene 7, lines 140 to 172

In these speeches how does Richard
use language first to show, and then
to hide, his true feelings?

18 marks

The text for the first extract (Richard's soliloquy: the introduction to the play) is reproduced on p.41. It has been highlighted and annotated to pick out the bits that relate to the question. It is very helpful to do this in the exam. You could then draw a spider diagram that focuses on language, but also considers themes and ideas, character and performance. Here is an incomplete spider diagram. What else could you add?

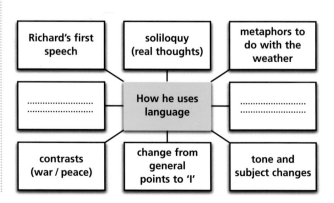

Then you should decide how to organise your essay. Here is one option:

- **Paragraph 1** - show you know what the question means. Include some general comments about the play as a whole.
- **Next paragraphs** - work through one speech and then the other, discussing aspects of Richard's language (especially how the language changes).
- **Concluding paragraph** - sum up your main points.

Alternatively, you could consider one aspect of his language at a time, comparing the two speeches as you go. This is more difficult, but could get you higher marks. You could start by numbering the points on the spider diagram as you decide in what order to make them.

Remember to use the **PEE** method for every point you make.

Extract from Richard lll, Act 1 Scene 1, lines 1-40

Now is the winter of our discontent
Made glorious summer by this son of York;
And all the clouds that loured upon our house
In the deep bosom of the ocean buried.
Now are our brows bound with victorious wreaths,　　5
Our bruisèd arms hung up for monuments,
Our stern alarums changed to merry meetings,
Our dreadful marches to delightful measures.
Grim-visaged war hath smoothed his wrinkled front,
And now – instead of mounting barbèd steeds　　10
To fright the souls of fearful adversaries –
He capers nimbly in a lady's chamber
To the lascivious pleasing of a lute.
But I, that am not shaped for sportive tricks
Nor made to court an amorous looking-glass,　　15
I that am rudely stamped and want love's majesty
To strut before a wanton ambling nymph,
I that am curtailed of this fair proportion,
Cheated of feature by dissembling nature,
Deformed, unfinished, sent before my time　　20
Into this breathing world scarce half made up –
And that so lamely and unfashionable
That dogs bark at me as I halt by them –
Why, I in this weak piping time of peace
Have no delight to pass away the time,　　25
Unless to spy my shadow in the sun
And descant on mine own deformity.
And therefore since I cannot prove a lover
To entertain these fair well-spoken days,
I am determinèd to prove a villain　　30
And hate the idle pleasures of these days.
Plots have I laid, inductions dangerous,
By drunken prophecies, libels and dreams,
To set my brother Clarence and the King
In deadly hate the one against the other.　　35
And if King Edward be as true and just
As I am subtle false and treacherous,
This day should Clarence closely be mewed up
About a prophecy which says that 'G'
Of Edward's heirs the murderer shall be.　　40

- Metaphors connected to weather

- Words about war and victory
- A series of contrasts (war and peace)

- War is personified as a soldier who now acts like a lover – the image sounds ridiculous, showing Richard's contempt

- Emphasis changes to Richard ('I'). He shows his real feelings

- Dwells on his physical appearance

- Repetition of 'I' reinforces focus

- Feels everything is against him

- Does not fit in

- Now he lets the audience know about the evil actions he intends to do

- Contrast

- Shows that he knows himself

A pun on the son of York (King Edward) and the sun

Alliteration of the letter 'm' sounds silly, contrast between heavy and light sounds

Nature is personified and held responsible

Reveals his true feelings about peace

'sun' refers back to the beginning

Does his birth and childhood explain his actions?

'G' could stand for George (Clarence's first name) or Gloucester (Richard's dukedom)

Shakespeare's Language

Below is a partial model answer to the question on the previous page. This answer deals only with the first of the two extracts.

1 The first speech comes at the very beginning of the play and introduces Richard's character to the audience. It is a soliloquy. Alone on stage, he speaks to the audience so we can assume that he is telling us his real thoughts and feelings.

2 First, he describes how England has changed now that the war is over and his brother, Edward, is king. It all seems very positive:

Now is the winter of our discontent
Made glorious summer by this son of York.

Here he uses metaphors that refer to the weather to show how great and positive the change is. He uses a pun to say that Edward (the son of York) is like the sun, bringing happiness and prosperity to his country.

3 He then uses a series of contrasts to illustrate the changes and he personifies 'grim-visag'd' war as an old soldier who now dances and sings. The use of alliteration ('merry meeting') helps make this sound rather ridiculous. His sarcasm tells us that Richard is not really happy with the way things are and makes the audience wonder why this is – after all, he is on the winning side.

4 Now the focus changes from England to his own position: 'But I, that am not shaped for sportive tricks'. This shows that he defines himself in terms of his physical deformity and feels that he does not fit in to the new, peaceful England. The repetition of 'I' reinforces this and indicates his selfishness. The audience now learns how he feels about being 'deformed, unfinished'.

5 His bitterness against 'dissembling Nature' could help to explain why he acts as he does later in the play. He feels like an outsider and wants revenge on the world. He too 'dissembles' or hides his nature. The audience might even feel some sympathy for him.

6 He ends by telling the audience what he intends to do (cause trouble between his two brothers) and how he will behave for the rest of the play: 'subtle, false and treacherous'. He also tells us that 'G' will be a murderer: 'G' could be George (Clarence) or Richard himself (Gloucester). It is almost as if he is teasing us and inviting us to keep watching to see what happens next.

Commentary on Model Answer

1
- Explains at what point in the play the speech is made (right at the beginning).
- We are told that it is a soliloquy and, more importantly, what this means (he talks to the audience) and what the significance of it is (he tells us what he really feels).
- Notice the use of 'the audience', showing that the writer is aware that the speech was written to be performed.

2
- The essay starts at the beginning of the speech and works its way through, commenting on language and meaning.
- Explains what Richard is saying (England has changed) and how he says it (using metaphors and a pun).
- Notice how PEE is used and how the two-line long quotation is laid out.

3
- Three features of language are noted: contrast, personification and alliteration. All these points are covered in just two sentences.
- Writer notes how these features give a certain 'tone' to the speech (sarcasm) and explains what this tone would tell the audience.
- Brief quotations are included within the sentences.

4
- The change in focus of the speech is discussed. This is important as it shows that the writer understands how the speech is structured, moving from one subject (England) to another (Richard).
- Again, the candidate explains what Richard means and how he uses language (the repetition of 'I').

5
- Shows an understanding of Richard's motivation: why he behaves as he does.
- The audience is mentioned again.

6
- Focus is on the last part of the speech (what Richard intends to do).
- It considers how he uses language to intrigue the audience (what does the prophecy mean?).
- It also concentrates on the effect of Richard's speech on the audience and how it sets us up for the rest of the play.

In the test, of course, you will be asked to discuss both of the extracts you have been given. You do not need to write the same amount about both extracts, however.

Ideas, Themes and Issues

Ideas, themes and issues questions are asking you what the play is about, and particularly what your set sections of the play are about. This does not mean writing about what happens in the scenes. If you simply re-tell the story (or plot) of the play, you will not be able to gain high marks, however well you tell it!

For this assessment focus you need to think about what matters to the writer, his characters and his audience. What is Shakespeare saying to the audience of his time and to us (the modern audience) about how people act, think and feel? What sort of world are they living in? What do they believe in? How are these ideas, themes and issues expressed in the play?

Whatever play you have studied, there will be certain ideas, themes and issues which you will have identified as being important to the whole play and which are present in the sections you have studied. Some themes that crop up frequently in Shakespeare's plays can be found alongside.

Some themes (such as ambition, revenge and the fatal flaw) are usually associated with tragedies or history plays, while others (such as love, marriage and forgiveness) are more usually found in the comedies and romances. However, many themes can be found expressed in different ways in different kinds of play.

Ambition	Kingship	Order and Chaos
War and Peace	Appearance and Reality	Guilt and Conscience
Good and Evil	Religion	Murder
Love	Marriage	Rebirth / Regeneration
The Supernatural / Magic	Deceit	Revenge
Parents and Children	Fate	Forgiveness
Betrayal	Friendship	Loyalty
Freedom	Nature and Nurture	Good Government
Masters and Servants	Jealousy	The Fatal Flaw

When you are considering the question you need to think about the ways in which these ideas, themes and issues are presented through…

- the characters' actions and speech
- their reactions to, and relationships with, other characters.

You should also think about Shakespeare's audiences and how their beliefs, knowledge and way of life may have influenced how they felt about what they saw on stage.

Religion and Beliefs

At the time that Shakespeare wrote, England was an overwhelmingly Christian country, so his audience would not only understand the many references to Christian beliefs in his plays, but would also probably share those beliefs. Yet many people also believed strongly in astrology and fate (beliefs disapproved of by the church), and believed that people have no control over what will happen to them because the course of their lives has already been decided.

Macbeth's killing of Duncan, for example, would have meant more to an audience in Shakespeare's time than the murder of an ordinary person because of the belief in the 'divine right of kings'. People believed that the king's authority came from God, so Macbeth would have been seen as defying God Himself. Witchcraft was also widely believed in, so the witches' power would have seemed much more real to them than it would to a modern audience.

Morals

In *Much Ado About Nothing*, Claudio's reaction to the (false) news that Hero has slept with another man might seem extreme to some modern audiences, but Shakespeare's original audience would have reacted in a similar way to Claudio because it was considered important for a woman to be a virgin when she married. The same idea is mentioned in *The Tempest* when Ferdinand first meets Miranda.

Context

The Tempest is often said to have been influenced by the experiences of English colonists who had settled in America and the West Indies. The way the newcomers to Prospero's island corrupt Caliban with drink might reflect how white settlers sometimes treated the native peoples they met. The question of whether or not Prospero is a good ruler might be answered differently by Jacobean and modern audiences.

There is not much doubt that both Elizabethan and modern audiences would consider Richard III, as portrayed by Shakespeare, to be a bad king. Shakespeare's interpretation of his character, however, might be very different from that of modern historians, because his sources would have been biased against Richard. That was because the real Richard had been overthrown by Henry VII, the grandfather of Queen Elizabeth I, so it suited the Tudors to paint him as a villain.

Ideas, Themes and Issues

■ Approaching the Question

This question focuses on ideas, themes and issues.

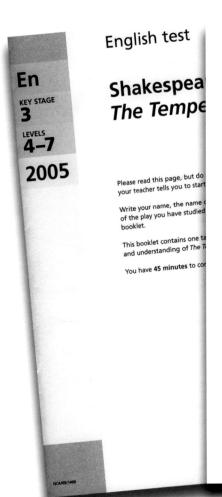

English test

En

KEY STAGE **3**

LEVELS **4–7**

2005

Shakespea
The Tempe

Please read this page, but do
your teacher tells you to start

Write your name, the name
of the play you have studied
booklet.

This booklet contains one ta
and understanding of *The T*

You have **45 minutes** to co

QCA/05/1409

The Tempest

Act 1 Scene 2, lines 320 to 374
Act 2 Scene 2, lines 134 to 171

In these scenes how does Shakespeare
explore attitudes to freedom and
slavery?

18 marks

The second extract is reproduced on the next page. In this extract, Stephano (the drunken butler) and Trinculo (the clown) have just met Caliban. Trinculo has offered him a drink. This time there are fewer comments in the margin. What other comments would you add?

Remember that although the focus of this question is the issue or theme of freedom and slavery, you also need to comment on language, character and the text in performance, focusing on how Shakespeare explores the theme.

When planning your answer, use your own preferred method. The example alongside uses headings with ideas jotted down under them. Make your own list and add anything else that occurs to you as you read the extract.

Remember to look for quotes that you can use to back up each point you make – PEE.

Freedom and Slavery
- Major theme of the play
- Ariel/Caliban
- Imprisonment
- Different masters – good and bad?
- Colonisation

Language
- Caliban – verse
- Others – prose
- Monster
- Repetition
- Descriptions of island

Characters
- Caliban – drunk, servant, resents Prospero, trusts newcomers
- Trinculo – jester, cynical commentator
- Stephano – drunken butler, servant-turned-master

Audience
- Sympathy for Caliban? Laugh at him?
- Knows about colonists, knows others alive
- Asides (Trinculo)

The Tempest, Act 2 Scene 2, lines 134–171

CALIBAN:	I'll show thee every fertile inch o'th' island,	
	And I will kiss thy foot. I prithee, be my god.	135
TRINCULO:	(*Aside*) By this light, a most perfidious and drunken	
	monster! When god's asleep, he'll rob his bottle.	
CALIBAN:	(*To* STEPHANO) I'll kiss thy foot. I'll swear myself thy subject.	
STEPHANO:	Come on then; down, and swear.	
	[CALIBAN *kneels*]	
TRINCULO:	(*Aside*) I shall laugh myself to death at this puppy-	140
	headed monster. A most scurvy monster! I could find	
	in my heart to beat him –	
STEPHANO:	(*To* CALIBAN) Come, kiss.	
	[CALIBAN *kisses his foot*]	
TRINCULO:	But that poor monster's in drink. An abominable monster!	
CALIBAN:	I'll show thee the best springs; I'll pluck thee berries;	145
	I'll fish for thee, and get thee wood enough.	
	A plague upon the tyrant that I serve!	
	I'll bear him no more sticks, but follow thee,	
	Thou wondrous man.	
TRINCULO:	(*Aside*) A most ridiculous monster, to make a wonder	150
	of a poor drunkard!	
CALIBAN:	(*To* STEPHANO) I prithee, let me bring thee where the crabs grow,	
	And I with my long nails will dig thee pig-nuts,	
	Show thee a jay's nest, and instruct thee how	
	To snare the nimble marmoset. I'll bring thee	155
	To clust'ring filberts, and sometimes I'll get thee	
	Young seamews from the rock. Wilt thou go with me?	
STEPHANO:	I prithee now, lead the way without any more	
	talking. – Trinculo, the King and all our company else	
	being drowned, we will inherit here. – Here, bear my	160
	bottle. – Fellow Trinculo, we'll fill him by and by again.	
CALIBAN:	(*Sings drunkenly*) Farewell, master, farewell, farewell!	
TRINCULO:	A howling monster, a drunken monster!	
CALIBAN:	(*Sings*) No more dams I'll make for fish,	
	Nor fetch in firing	165
	At requiring,	
	Nor scrape trenchering, nor wash dish.	
	'Ban, 'ban, Cacaliban	
	Has a new master. – Get a new man!	
	Freedom, high-day! High-day, freedom!	170
	Freedom, high-day, freedom!	

Margin annotations:
- Offers to be their guide
- Comments to audience
- Wants to be their slave
- Repetition of 'monster'
- Strong theatrical gesture
- Sympathy?
- Hatred for Prospero / Recalls Miranda
- Poetic description
- Dramatic irony – they are alive
- They corrupt him with drink
- Entertaining, comical, pathetic / Rejects 'good master' for a worse fate

Ideas, Themes and Issues

Model Answer

This part of the answer focuses on Act 2 Scene 2.

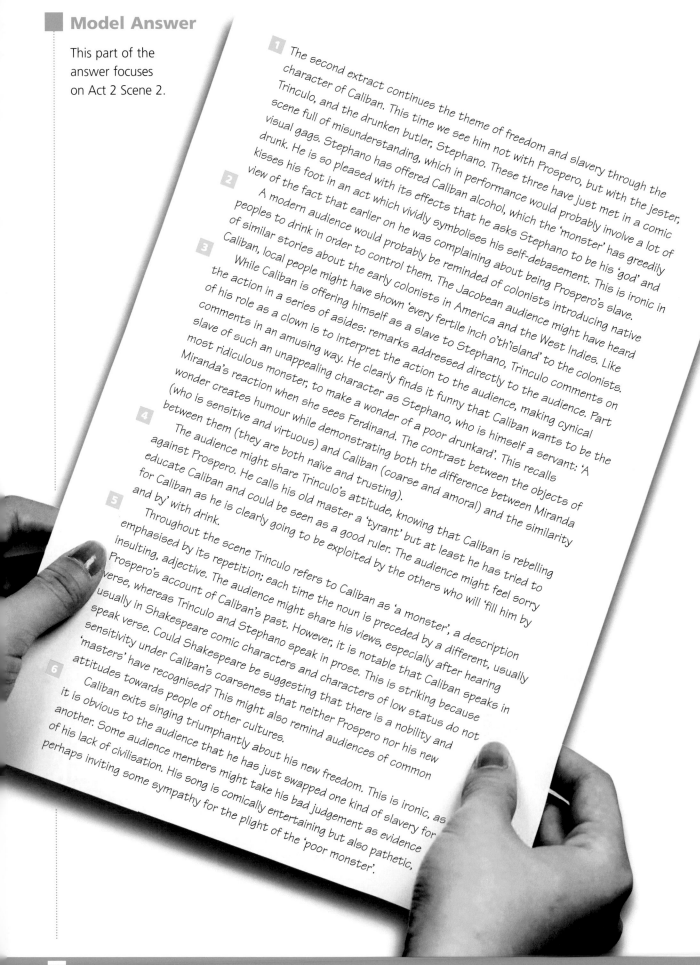

1 The second extract continues the theme of freedom and slavery through the character of Caliban. This time we see him not with Prospero, but with the jester, Trinculo, and the drunken butler, Stephano. These three have just met in a comic scene full of misunderstanding, which in performance would probably involve a lot of visual gags. Stephano has offered Caliban alcohol, which the 'monster' has greedily drunk. He is so pleased with its effects that he asks Stephano to be his 'god' and

2 kisses his foot in an act which vividly symbolises his self-debasement. This is ironic in view of the fact that earlier on he was complaining about being Prospero's slave. A modern audience would probably be reminded of colonists introducing native peoples to drink in order to control them. The Jacobean audience might have heard of similar stories about the early colonists in America and the West Indies. Like

3 Caliban, local people might have shown 'every fertile inch o'th'island' to the colonists. While Caliban is offering himself as a slave to Stephano, Trinculo comments on the action in a series of asides: remarks addressed directly to the audience, making cynical comments in an amusing way. He clearly finds it funny that Caliban wants to be the slave of such an unappealing character as Stephano, who is himself a servant: 'A most ridiculous monster, to make a wonder of a poor drunkard'. This recalls Miranda's reaction when she sees Ferdinand. The contrast between the objects of wonder creates humour while demonstrating both the difference between Miranda

4 (who is sensitive and virtuous) and Caliban (coarse and amoral) and the similarity between them (they are both naïve and trusting). The audience might share Trinculo's attitude, knowing that Caliban is rebelling against Prospero. He calls his old master a 'tyrant' but at least he has tried to educate Caliban and could be seen as a good ruler. The audience might feel sorry for Caliban as he is clearly going to be exploited by the others who will 'fill him

5 and by' with drink. Throughout the scene Trinculo refers to Caliban as 'a monster', a description emphasised by its repetition; each time the noun is preceded by a different, usually insulting, adjective. The audience might share his views, especially after hearing Prospero's account of Caliban's past. However, it is notable that Caliban speaks in verse, whereas Trinculo and Stephano speak in prose. This is striking because usually in Shakespeare comic characters and characters of low status do not speak verse. Could Shakespeare be suggesting that there is a nobility and sensitivity under Caliban's coarseness that neither Prospero nor his new

6 'masters' have recognised? This might also remind audiences of common attitudes towards people of other cultures. Caliban exits singing triumphantly about his new freedom. This is ironic, as it is obvious to the audience that he has just swapped one kind of slavery for another. Some audience members might take his bad judgement as evidence of his lack of civilisation. His song is comically entertaining but also pathetic, perhaps inviting some sympathy for the plight of the 'poor monster'.

Commentary on Model Answer

This answer focuses very clearly on the themes of freedom and slavery, but also shows awareness of the other three assessment focuses: language, character and text in performance. The words 'freedom' and 'slavery' are mentioned in the first sentence and a glance through the rest of the essay shows that the writer uses words connected with this theme in every paragraph.

1
- The writer will have already written about the first extract. This paragraph links the two extracts, saying that the second 'continues the theme' and refers to the other scene.
- The writer shows understanding of the relationships between the characters.
- There is awareness of the text in performance, shown in the references to the 'visual gags' and to the significance of Caliban kissing Stephano's foot.

2
- Shows knowledge of the play's social and historical background by explaining the connection with the experiences of colonists in Shakespeare's time.
- Also mentions the audience.

3
- Trinculo's asides, an important dramatic technique in the extract, are discussed.
- His role as a typical Shakespearean clown is commented on. This again shows an understanding of historical context as well as of the text in performance.
- The writer stresses the comedy of the scene as well as its relevance to the themes of freedom and slavery.

- The quotation leads into an explanation that links the scene to the rest of the play and gives an interesting insight into two of the main characters (Miranda and Caliban) by comparing their reactions to meeting the shipwrecked men.

4
- Possible audience reactions are mentioned (not for the first time).
- Note how reactions are linked to the issues mentioned in the question.
- The word 'might' is used, showing that the writer realises that different audiences could react in different ways.

5
- An important aspect of language (verse and prose) is discussed, but the themes, ideas and issues are kept in the foreground.
- The significance of Caliban speaking in verse is explored in the light of the question. The writer again discusses possible interpretations, rather than answers.
- Remember English is not about 'finding the right answer'. There are many possible answers. The important thing is that your answer is written convincingly and backed up by evidence from the text.

6
- The final paragraph deals with the action at the end of the extract.
- It highlights that although Caliban is still a slave because he has a new master, he considers himself to be free. It discusses how the audience might react to him as well.

The Text in Performance

Directing and Acting Advice

Questions on this aspect of Shakespeare's plays are quite different from questions on the other three assessment focuses, but this makes them easy to spot. Don't be intimidated by them. You do not need to have directed a play or even acted in one to be able to answer these questions successfully. You simply have to demonstrate your knowledge and understanding of the play in a slightly different way.

You may be asked how you would **direct** the given extract, possibly focussing on creating a certain **mood** or **atmosphere**, or you may be asked specifically what advice you, as the director, would give to an actor playing a certain part. You might even be asked to write about how you would interpret a part if you were the actor.

If it asks you to imagine you are the director, write as if you are the person who decides what happens on stage: in other words, how the scene is interpreted by the actors. You can use phrases such as 'I would advise the actor to...', 'at this point he could...' and 'I

would ask her to...'. For example, in a scene where two lovers are scared of their families finding out about their affair, you could say...

> I would advise the actors to stand close to each other, holding hands to show their closeness. I would ask them to whisper their lines to show that they are scared of being overheard. They could look around furtively from time to time, as if they think someone might find them.

If you are asked to write as an actor it is very important that you do not just state what you should be doing, but explain why you should be doing it. In this way you relate everything you say to the meaning of the text and the other assessment focuses. You can use phrases such as 'I would', 'I could' and 'I might'. For example, if you were playing a young lover and you were asked how you might act in a scene where you are being confronted by your lover's father, you could write...

> At this point I would pace on the stage from left to right. I might repeat some words and stumble over others. This would show that I am nervous.

Creating Mood and Atmosphere

Instead of asking you to give advice to actors, a question on the text in performance could ask you how you would create a mood and / or an atmosphere. Some of the effects you could be asked to create could include…

- a threatening mood
- a playful mood
- a tense atmosphere
- a romantic mood.

Sound effects can convey mood very effectively. For example, in the scene where Macbeth is worried about the forthcoming battle, you could increase the war-like atmosphere by having the sound of drums or the shouts of soldiers off-stage. In *The Tempest* you could use the sounds of the sea and the wind to indicate the danger the sailors are in.

Music can also be used. For example, solemn church music could set the scene for Claudio and Hero's

wedding in *Much Ado About Nothing* or triumphant military music could be played before Richard enters in the first scene in *Richard III*. This would indicate that there has been a war and that Richard's side has won.

Lighting can be a very useful tool to create or change a mood. Bright lights often reflect a happy, joyful mood. Dimming the lights at a certain point in the scene could increase a sense of danger or fear, or it could just show that the sun is setting. For example, you could dim the lights when the mood changes from joy to anger and sorrow when Claudio refuses to marry Hero in *Much Ado About Nothing*. You can use a spotlight when you want the audience to concentrate on a particular actor, perhaps someone who is speaking in a soliloquy; for example, when Richard performs his opening speech in *Richard III*.

Colours can also be significant. The colour of the scenery and the lighting used can help to set the mood. Blue lights usually create a cold, unfriendly atmosphere, while pinks and reds can help to make a scene warmer.

The Text in Performance

Actors interpret the text vocally and physically. You must think about how they speak their lines, what they do while speaking and how they relate to other actors on the stage.

Conveying Meaning Through Speech

Volume of speech can range from a whisper to a shout. If an actor raises his voice, perhaps even starts shouting, this could represent an attempt to assert his authority, or it could show that he is angry, or he could simply be trying to gain the attention of a large number of people. When people lower their voices, perhaps to a whisper, it could be because they are sharing a secret, threatening someone or feeling exhausted. The volume of the line delivered will also affect how the other actors react.

Tone is the way lines are delivered. Asking an actor to speak lines a certain way can change the whole tone of a scene. The tone could be depressing, menacing, sarcastic or even neutral to convey a range of emotions.

Speed is how quickly actors speak and can be very significant. 'Gabbled' or rushed speech can be a sign of nervousness, while talking slowly and evenly can convey authority.

Emphasis is the extra stress put on certain words to highlight their importance. Changing which words are emphasised can really change the tone of the sentence.

Pauses are the absence of speech and can be equally as important as words. A lot of thought goes into when actors should **pause** and how long a pause should be. An actor might pause to emphasise the importance of what has just been said, to give it time to sink in. He could pause to show his character is uncertain about what to say next, or to show that he is thinking about something. Also, an actor will sometimes pause before speaking to give himself time to react to what has just been said or done: perhaps to show shock, surprise or disbelief.

Conveying Meaning Through Body Language

Facial expressions are important when showing the audience what characters are feeling at any given moment – or what they want the other characters to think they are feeling. You might ask an actor to grin broadly in a show of happiness and confidence, to raise their eyebrows to show surprise, or to look at the ground to show shyness. Whether or not characters make **eye contact** with each other can tell us a lot about their relationships as well. Think about how an actor could show anger, sorrow, untrustworthiness or innocence.

Body language can also betray a character's true feelings or emotions. How someone stands can be significant: shifting from one foot to another can betray nervousness, while standing still and straight can show confidence. They way people walk, too, can tell us something about them: from their age, to their mood to their status. Body language also includes gestures, such as pointing at people to intimidate them perhaps, or putting a hand over one's mouth to express shock.

Physical closeness or distance between actors on stage can also tell the audience a lot about the characters' relationships. Closeness can convey a variety of things, from emotional intimacy to intimidation. Distance between actors might show that they are wary of each other, that they have had an argument or that one is asserting authority over the other.

Conveying Status

Status means how important someone is. A king or queen would normally have a high status, while a servant would have low status.

People's status can vary according to how confident or happy they are, or what other characters on stage might feel about them. For example, in *Much Ado About Nothing*, Hero has a high social status, but when she is humiliated on her wedding day, she becomes an object of pity or disapproval and therefore has a low status. Stephano in *The Tempest* is a servant and would normally have low status, but when he gets Caliban drunk he becomes important in Caliban's eyes and acquires high status.

Position on stage can be used to show status. Levels might be used, where the actor who has a higher status is on a physically higher level. An actor who is upstage (towards the back of the stage) usually has higher status than one who is downstage (at the front).

Costume can also be used to convey character and status. For example, how would Macbeth and Lady Macbeth dress when they become King and Queen of Scotland? How could the plight of the shipwrecked characters in *The Tempest* be reflected in the state of their clothes?

The Text in Performance

Here is a question that focuses on the text in performance.

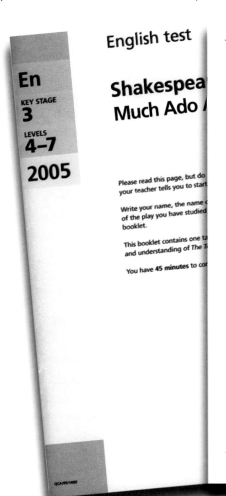

English test

En
KEY STAGE
3
LEVELS
4–7
2005

Shakespea
Much Ado

Please read this page, but do
your teacher tells you to start

Write your name, the name
of the play you have studied
booklet.

This booklet contains one ta
and understanding of *The T*

You have **45 minutes** to co

QCA/05/1409

Much Ado About Nothing

Act 3 Scene 2, lines 73 to 125
Act 4 Scene 1, lines 10 to 60

Imagine that you are directing these scenes for
a school production. What advice would you
give to the actor playing Claudio?

The best approach to this sort of question is to work through the extract line by line, making notes on the text as you go. The second extract (on the facing page) has been annotated with directions for Claudio. In this extract Claudio and Hero (the daughter of Leonato) are about to be married, but Claudio has been told that Hero has been seen with another man.

The brief paragraph plan (alongside) is based on the comments on the extract. It follows the order of the scene and considers what advice would be given to the actor playing Claudio at each stage of the scene. You might start a new paragraph when there is a change in the character's mood or when something significant occurs.

Remember that you must say why you want the actor to act and react in a certain way. Otherwise, the examiner will not be able to tell whether you understand the play or not.

Paragraph Plan

At the start - formal (wedding picture) – still, watching and waiting. Audience knows what Claudio has been told.

Shock of his answer to the friar. Reasonable, even tone - keeps Hero in the dark, creating tension.

Sudden angry reaction changes mood of scene.

Claudio takes control and accuses Hero. Reactions.

Leonato tries to calm the situation - makes Claudio angrier. He 'spells it out'. Takes the moral highground. Anger reaches a climax. Physically violent to her? Shocks characters and audience.

Conclusion - how the audience would react to Claudio.

Much Ado About Nothing, Act 4 Scene 1, lines 10–60

FRIAR:	If either of you know any inward impediment why you should not be conjoined, I charge you on your souls to utter it.	10
CLAUDIO:	Know you any, Hero?	
HERO:	None, my lord.	
FRIAR:	Know you any, Count?	15
LEONATO:	I dare make his answer none.	
CLAUDIO:	O, what men dare do! What men may do! What men daily do, not knowing what they do!	
BENEDICK:	How now! Interjections? Why then, some be of laughing, as, 'ah, ha, he!'	20
CLAUDIO:	Stand thee by, Friar. Father, by your leave, Will you with free and unconstrainèd soul Give me this maid, your daughter?	
LEONATO:	As freely, son, as God did give her me.	
CLAUDIO:	And what have I to give you back whose worth May counterpoise this rich and precious gift?	25
DON PEDRO:	Nothing, unless you render her again.	
CLAUDIO:	Sweet Prince, you learn me noble thankfulness. There, Leonato, take her back again. Give not this rotten orange to your friend. .... Would you not swear, All of you that see her, that she were a maid, By these exterior shows? But she is none. She knows the heat of a luxurious bed. Her blush is guiltiness, not modesty.	30 ...36 40
LEONATO:	What do you mean, my lord?	
CLAUDIO:	Not to be married, Not to knit my soul to an approvèd wanton.	
LEONATO:	Dear my lord, if you in your own proof Have vanquished the resistance of her youth And made defeat of her virginity -	45
CLAUDIO:	I know what you would say. If I have known her, You will say she did embrace me as a husband, And so extenuate the 'forehand sin. No, Leonato, I never tempted her with word too large, But, as a brother to his sister, showed Bashful sincerity and comely love.	50
HERO:	And seemed I ever otherwise to you?	
CLAUDIO:	Out on thee! Seeming! I will write against it; You seem to me as Dian in her orb, As chaste as is the bud ere it be blown; But you are more intemperate in your blood Than Venus, or those pampered animals That rage in savage sensuality.	55 60

these dotted lines show a section of this speech has been cut

- angry, loud, gesturing

- shakes him off
- ignores others
- takes control

- seems innocent

- looks at Prince
- gracious
- pushes her to him?
- treats her as an object
- contempt
- disbelieving

- impatient

- tries to calm situation, misunderstanding

- dismissive

- authoritative pause

moral 'highground'

she comes to him anger flares up physical violence?

disgust and contempt

The Text in Performance

■ Model Answer

This is a partial answer to the question on the previous page.

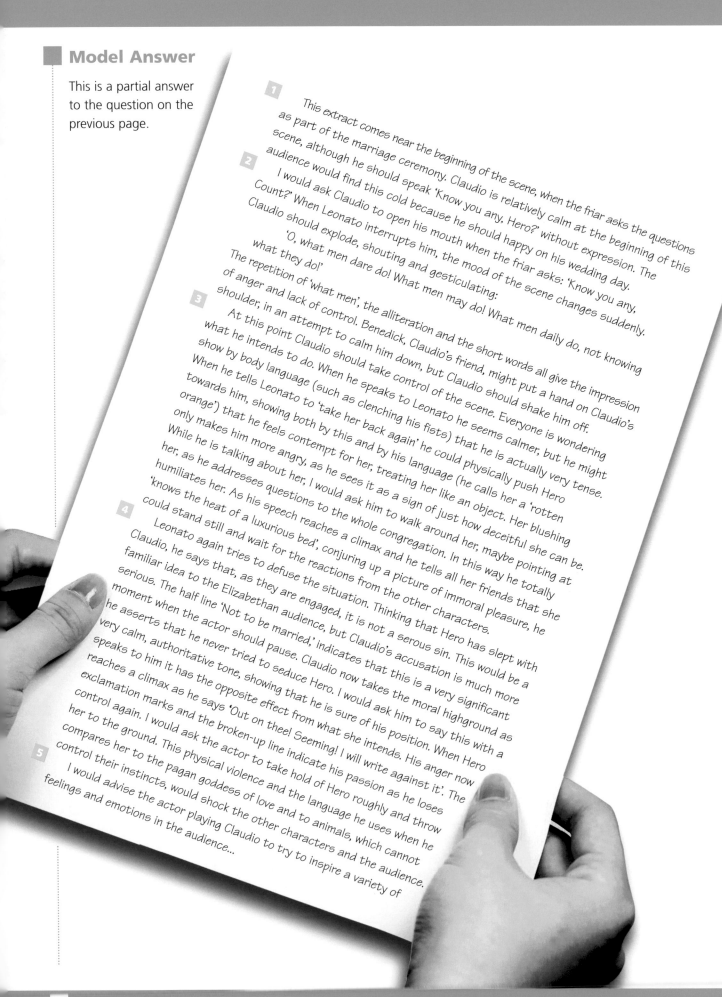

1 This extract comes near the beginning of the scene, when the friar asks the questions as part of the marriage ceremony. Claudio is relatively calm at the beginning of this scene, although he should speak 'Know you any, Hero?' without expression. The audience would find this cold because he should happy on his wedding day.

2 I would ask Claudio to open his mouth when the friar asks: 'Know you any, Count?' When Leonato interrupts him, the mood of the scene changes suddenly. Claudio should explode, shouting and gesticulating:

'O, what men dare do! What men may do! What men daily do, not knowing what they do!'

3 The repetition of 'what men', the alliteration and the short words all give the impression of anger and lack of control. Benedick, Claudio's friend, might put a hand on Claudio's shoulder, in an attempt to calm him down, but Claudio should shake him off.

At this point Claudio should take control of the scene. When he speaks to Leonato he seems calmer, but he might show by body language (such as clenching his fists) that he is actually very tense. When he tells Leonato to 'take her back again' he could physically push Hero towards him, showing both by this and by his language (he calls her a 'rotten orange') that he feels contempt for her, treating her like an object. Her blushing only makes him more angry, as he sees it as a sign of just how deceitful she can be. While he is talking about her, I would ask him to walk around her, maybe pointing at her, as he addresses questions to the whole congregation. In this way he totally humiliates her. As his speech reaches a climax and he tells all her friends that she 'knows the heat of a luxurious bed', conjuring up a picture of immoral pleasure, he could stand still and wait for the reactions from the other characters.

4 Leonato again tries to defuse the situation. Thinking that Hero has slept with Claudio, he says that, as they are engaged, it is not a serous sin. This would be a familiar idea to the Elizabethan audience, but Claudio's accusation is much more serious. The half line 'Not to be married,' indicates that this is a very significant moment when the actor should pause. Claudio now takes the moral highground as he asserts that he never tried to seduce Hero. I would ask him to say this with a very calm, authoritative tone, showing that he is sure of his position. When Hero speaks to him it has the opposite effect from what she intends. His anger now reaches a climax as he says 'Out on thee! Seeming! I will write against it'. The exclamation marks and the broken-up line indicate his passion as he loses control again. I would ask the actor to take hold of Hero roughly and throw her to the ground. This physical violence and the language he uses when he

5 compares her to the pagan goddess of love and to animals, which cannot control their instincts, would shock the other characters and the audience.

I would advise the actor playing Claudio to try to inspire a variety of feelings and emotions in the audience...

Commentary on Model Answer

1
- This paragraph would come after a discussion of the first set extract and a paragraph linking the two extracts, which would explain how things are at the beginning of the scene. It might suggest that Claudio and the others stand in a very formal arrangement, Claudio keeping his thoughts to himself, or it could suggest that he feels betrayed. Both interpretations are valid.
- Audience is mentioned. It is important to keep mentioning the audience's possible reactions (e.g. 'shock') because performance is about communicating with an audience.

2
- This paragraph shows that the candidate understands the mood of the scene and how it changes.
- Although the focus of the answer is Claudio, it also mentions the effect of his speech and actions on other characters.
- The other characters' actions and speech and their effect on Claudio are discussed.
- Language is touched on ('alliteration… short words').
- Suggestions are included to advise the actor how to speak ('shouting') and what physical actions to use, e.g. 'gesticulating'.
- The writer always makes it clear why characters act as they do (characters' motivation), e.g. 'in an attempt to calm him down'.

3
- The focus is on Claudio's control of the scene and explains how an actor could show his state of mind to an audience.
- Mood (calmness), body language (clenching fists), attitude (contempt), physical contact with another actor (pushing Hero), movement and stillness (walking around her) and gestures (pointing) are all discussed.

4
- The focus is still on Claudio's performance, but there is also an awareness of social and historical context (what an Elizabethan audience might have thought) and of the main themes of the play (honour, trust, appearance and reality).
- The suggestion that the actor should throw Hero to the ground is justified by an analysis of the language of his speech.
- Notice how the writer has saved this most dramatic action for the climax of the scene.

5
- You could finish the essay by summing up the mixture of emotions that the actor's performance might inspire and showing an understanding of what the scene is about and how that can be conveyed in performance.

Remember – you can direct your actor to do anything as long as you can explain **why** you want him to do it and what it will tell the audience. This is what shows that you understand the text and is what will gain you marks.

Character and Motivation

The word **character** is used to describe a person in a play. It also means what sort of person someone is. You can talk about someone's 'characteristics': whether a person is an optimist or pessimist; kind hearted or cruel; vain or modest etc. When the test question asks you to discuss characters in a play you need to think about what sort of people they are, how they behave and what the audience would think about them. You will also have to consider their motivation. **Motivation** simply means why people do the things they do.

The main ways in which we learn about characters are through…
- what they say
- what others say about them and to them
- how they act and react.

These are looked at in more detail below.

What They Say

People do not always tell the truth about themselves or their motivation. Shakespeare's plays are full of people who lie, cheat and deceive, like Don John in *Much Ado About Nothing*, Richard in *Richard III* and Antonio in *The Tempest*.

Fortunately, you do not have to guess whether or not Shakespeare's characters are telling the truth. Shakespeare liked his audience to know what was really going on, so he made it clear when his characters could not be trusted.

Sometimes we know what they are up to because they may have discussed their plans with a close friend or 'confidant' in a previous scene. For example, the audience knows that Lady Macbeth is insincere when she welcomes Duncan into her house because she has advised her husband to 'look like the innocent flower / But be the serpent under't' (*Macbeth* Act 1 Scene 5).

At other times the characters tell others what they have done, as in *Much Ado About Nothing* when Borachio tells Conrade about the plot to disgrace Hero, confiding that it was planned by Don John, whom he calls 'the devil, my master' (Act 3 Scene 3).

We know what Richard is up to in *Richard III* because he tells us directly in a soliloquy. A **soliloquy** is a speech made by a character directly to the audience, often when there is nobody else present on stage. If a Shakespearean character speaks to us directly we know that we are hearing the truth. When Richard delivers his famous speech beginning 'Now is the winter of our discontent' (*Richard III* Act 1 Scene 1) or Macbeth asks 'Is this a dagger that I see before me?' (*Macbeth* Act 2 Scene 1) it is almost as if we are reading their minds. They tell us what they really think and how they really feel. They tell us why they do the things they do.

What Other Characters Say About Them and To Them

Just as in real life, different characters have different opinions of each other. As we have seen, some of Shakespeare's characters are very deceitful and fool those around them, at least for a time. For example, Richard lll is so successful in deceiving people that Buckingham tells him that he should be king.

At the beginning of *Macbeth* everybody is so full of praise for Macbeth – praise he deserves – that when he kills the king, the other characters do not realise that he has changed and do not suspect him of the murder. Later on, however, when people begin to see through them, Macbeth and Lady Macbeth are called names such as 'tyrant', 'devil' and 'fiend'.

Sometimes we get different (and opposing) messages about the same character. In *The Tempest* most characters think of Prospero as a good ruler and a good man, but to Caliban he is a 'tyrant'. Caliban feels that he has been cruelly treated; yet to Miranda and Prospero, Caliban is an evil creature who has abused their kindness.

An audience might be able to see both points of view. If you know that there are differing views of a character, mention them, and comment on why one character might hold a particular view of another character.

How They Act and React

The main way in which we learn about characters' behaviour in a play is by seeing it. Even if characters lie to other characters, the audience can see what they actually do and judge them accordingly. Sometimes this can mean very important actions which form the plot of the play. For example, Macbeth kills King Duncan, which the audience knows is a dreadful crime. He then goes on to have Banquo, his best friend, murdered and even kills the innocent wife and children of Macduff. By the time he has done this, the audience will have little or no sympathy for him.

You can also learn a lot about characters from their actions within a scene. When we see Lady Macbeth washing her hands over and over again, we know that her conscience has finally caught up with her. Likewise, when Caliban kisses the drunken Stephano's foot in *The Tempest*, he demonstrates both his servility and his lack of judgement.

We know a lot about Prospero's magical powers in *The Tempest* because we see him using them. We also see why he uses them: to bring people to justice, but also

to forgive and reconcile. This tells us a lot about his character.

Sometimes the fact that a character says very little can have an impact on the audience, such as Hero's reaction to Claudio when he refuses to marry her. Perhaps she is unable to say much because she is so surprised and shocked. When she faints it tells us a lot about the sort of character she is and the seriousness of what has happened.

To prepare yourself for the test questions, think about which characters you think you might be asked about. They will be important characters who have a lot to say and do in the scenes you have studied. Here is a typical question about character and motivation.

Macbeth

Act 2 Scene 1, lines 20 to the end
Act 5 Scene 5, lines 15 to the end

What do you learn from these extracts about Macbeth's character and motivation and how they have changed during the play?

You could draw a grid (such as the one below) to plan this question. Read the two extracts on the following pages and see if you can add to the grid before reading the Model Answer (p.62). In the first extract Macbeth is about to murder King Duncan (p.60) and Banquo reminds Macbeth of the witches' prophecy. In the second extract (p.61) Macbeth is preparing for battle with the invading armies of Malcolm and Macduff and he hears a cry from the castle.

Macbeth	First extract	Second extract
What he says	• Horrific imagery - aware of what he is doing	• He is looking forward to death • He doesn't care any more • He will go out fighting
What others say		• Message about the wood - reminds him of the prophecy
How he acts and reacts	• He tries to grasp the dagger • He follows the dagger to murder Duncan	

Character and Motivation

Macbeth, Act 2 Scene 1, lines 20–65.

BANQUO:	I dreamt last night of the three weird sisters. 20
	To you they have showed some truth.
MACBETH:	I think not of them;
	Yet, when we can entreat an hour to serve,
	We would spend it in some words upon that business,
	If you would grant the time.
BANQUO:	At your kind'st leisure.
MACBETH:	If you shall cleave to my consent when 'tis, 25
	It shall make honour for you.
BANQUO:	So I lose none
	In seeking to augment it, but still keep
	My bosom franchised and allegiance clear,
	I shall be counselled.
MACBETH:	Good repose the while. 30
BANQUO:	Thanks, sir. The like to you. [*Exeunt* BANQUO *and* FLEANCE]
MACBETH:	(*To the* SERVANT) Go bid thy mistress, when my drink is ready,
	She strike upon the bell. Get thee to bed. [*Exit* SERVANT]
	Is this a dagger which I see before me,
	The handle toward my hand? Come, let me clutch thee. 35
	I have thee not, and yet I see thee still.
	Art thou not, fatal vision, sensible
	To feeling as to sight? Or art thou but
	A dagger of the mind, a false creation
	Proceeding from the heat-oppressèd brain? 40
	I see thee yet, in form as palpable
	As this which now I draw.
	Thou marshall'st me the way that I was going,
	And such an instrument I was to use.
	Mine eyes are made the fools o'th' other senses, 45
	Or else worth all the rest. I see thee still,
	And on thy blade and dudgeon gouts of blood,
	Which was not so before. There's no such thing.
	It is the bloody business which informs
	Thus to mine eyes. Now o'er the one-half world 50
	Nature seems dead, and wicked dreams abuse
	The curtained sleep. Witchcraft celebrates
	Pale Hecate's offerings, and withered murder,
	Alarumed by his sentinel the wolf,
	Whose howl's his watch, thus with his stealthy pace, 55
	With Tarquin's ravishing strides, towards his design
	Moves like a ghost… 57
	…Whiles I threat, he lives. …61
	Words to the heat of deeds too cold breath gives. [*A bell rings*]
	I go, and it is done. The bell invites me.
	Hear it not, Duncan; for it is a knell
	That summons thee to heaven or to hell. 65

these ellipses show that a section of the speech has been cut

Macbeth, Act 5 Scene 5, lines 15 to end.

MACBETH: Wherefore was that cry?   15

SEYTON: The Queen, my lord, is dead.

MACBETH: She should have died hereafter.

There would have been a time for such a word.

Tomorrow, and tomorrow, and tomorrow

Creeps in this petty pace from day to day   20

To the last syllable of recorded time,

And all our yesterdays have lighted fools

The way to dusty death. Out, out, brief candle.

Life's but a walking shadow, a poor player

That struts and frets his hour upon the stage,   25

And then is heard no more. It is a tale

Told by an idiot, full of sound and fury,

Signifying nothing.

                     [*Enter a* MESSENGER]

Thou com'st to use Thy tongue: thy story quickly.

MESSENGER: Gracious my lord, I should report that which I saw,   30

But know not how to do't.

MACBETH: Well, say, sir.

MESSENGER: As I did stand my watch upon the hill

I looked toward Birnam, and anon methought

The wood began to move.

MACBETH: Liar and slave!

MESSENGER: Let me endure your wrath, if't be not so.   35

Within this three mile you may see it coming;

I say a moving grove.

MACBETH: If thou speak'st false

Upon the next tree shalt thou hang alive

Till famine cling thee. If thy speech be sooth,

I care not if thou dost for me as much.   40

I pall in resolution, and begin

To doubt th'equivocation of the fiend,

That lies like truth. 'Fear not till Birnam Wood

Do come to Dunsinane' – and now a wood

Comes toward Dunsinane. Arm, arm and out.   45

If this which he avouches does appear

There is nor flying hence nor tarrying here.

I 'gin to be aweary of the sun,

And wish th'estate o'th' world were now undone.

Ring the alarum bell. [*Alarums*] Blow wind, come wrack,   50

At least we'll die with harness on our back.

Character and Motivation

Model Answer

This partial answer covers both extracts mentioned in the question. However, two paragraphs have been omitted. You could have a go at writing them yourself.

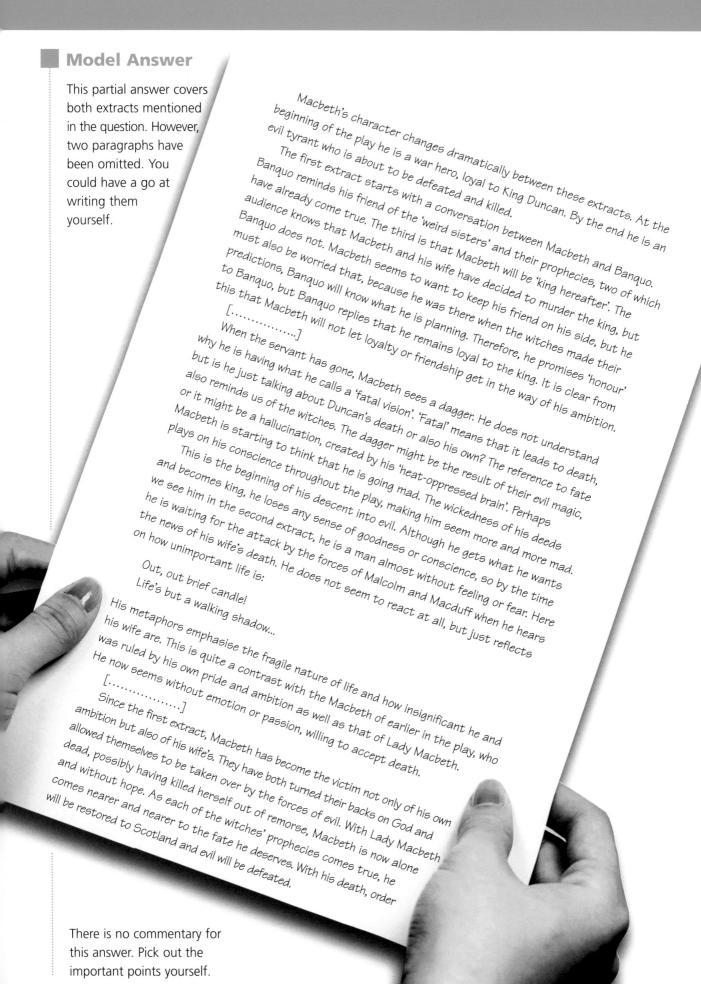

Macbeth's character changes dramatically between these extracts. At the beginning of the play he is a war hero, loyal to King Duncan. By the end he is an evil tyrant who is about to be defeated and killed.

The first extract starts with a conversation between Macbeth and Banquo. Banquo reminds his friend of the 'weird sisters' and their prophecies, two of which have already come true. The third is that Macbeth and his wife will be 'king hereafter'. The audience knows that Macbeth does not. Macbeth seems to want to have decided to murder the king, but Banquo does not. Macbeth seems to want to keep his friend on his side, but he must also be worried that, because he was there when the witches made their predictions, Banquo will know what he is planning. Therefore, he promises 'honour' to Banquo, but Banquo replies that he remains loyal to the king. It is clear from this that Macbeth will not let loyalty or friendship get in the way of his ambition.

[. . . . .]

When the servant has gone, Macbeth sees a dagger. He does not understand why he is having what he calls a 'fatal vision'. 'Fatal' means that it leads to death, but is he just talking about Duncan's death or also his own? The reference to fate also reminds us of the witches. The dagger might be the result of their evil magic, or it might be a hallucination, created by his 'heat-oppressed brain'. Perhaps Macbeth is starting to think that he is going mad. The wickedness of his deeds plays on his conscience throughout the play, making him seem more and more mad. This is the beginning of his descent into evil. Although he gets what he wants and becomes king, he loses any sense of goodness or conscience, so by the time we see him in the second extract, he is a man almost without feeling or fear. Here he is waiting for the attack by the forces of Malcolm and Macduff when he hears the news of his wife's death. He does not seem to react at all, but just reflects on how unimportant life is:

> Out, out brief candle!
> Life's but a walking shadow...

His metaphors emphasise the fragile nature of life and how insignificant he and his wife are. This is quite a contrast with the Macbeth of earlier in the play, who was ruled by his own pride and ambition as well as that of Lady Macbeth. He now seems without emotion or passion, willing to accept death.

[. . . . .]

Since the first extract, Macbeth has become the victim not only of his own ambition but also of his wife's. They have both turned their backs on God and allowed themselves to be taken over by the forces of evil. With Lady Macbeth dead, possibly having killed herself out of remorse, Macbeth is now alone and without hope. As each of the witches' prophecies comes true, he comes nearer and nearer to the fate he deserves. With his death, order will be restored to Scotland and evil will be defeated.

There is no commentary for this answer. Pick out the important points yourself.

Empathy Questions

An **empathy** question is a particular kind of character and motivation question. You need to write as if you were a character in the play.

Approaching the Question

An empathy question on Macbeth might read:

> Imagine you are Macbeth. Explain how and why your feelings have changed between the two extracts.

Questions like this require you to show that you understand how Shakespeare uses language and dramatic skill to give life to his characters and explore the themes of the play. There is a little more scope for you to use your imagination, but do not create your own version of characters and events – your answer must be rooted in the text!

Here are some things to think about if you are given an empathy question. You should...

- write as if you were the character ('I...')
- think about your status; if you are Macbeth you become king between the two extracts
- think about your relationships with other characters: as Macbeth you would need to explain your odd reaction to your wife's death
- remember that you might not be aware of everything that the audience knows about, e.g. Macbeth does not know that Malcolm's army has cut branches from the wood to make camouflage
- make sure that you use quotations from the text.

Model Answer

You should plan your answer just as you would plan any answer that focuses on character. Then you should write your answer, remembering to write as if you were that character. Here is an extract from an answer to the question on Macbeth. Macbeth is reflecting on his conversation with Banquo.

> After my wife had persuaded me - with her taunting and arguments - that I should murder the king, I met Banquo. He was about to leave the castle with his son, Fleance. Banquo reminded me of when we met the 'weird sisters' and their prophecies, two of which had already come true. The third was that I would be 'king hereafter'. This worried me because, knowing what the witches had said, he might have guessed what I was planning. So, without giving anything away, I promised 'honour' to Banquo in the future, but he left me in no doubt that he was loyal to the king. I had already decided I would not let loyalty or morality get in the way of my ambition and now I decided that I would not let friendship get in my way either. The witches told Banquo he would 'get kings', meaning his descendants would be kings. I could not let that happen.

Compare it to the second paragraph of the model answer on p.62. Note how the content of this answer is very similar to the answer to the non-empathy question. It is just expressed in a different way.

Revision and Test Tips

Revision Tips

- Read a summary of the play or watch a video to remind yourself of the story and how your scenes fit into it.
- Read through any notes you have been given in class.
- Try to think of possible questions on your scenes, at least one for each 'assessment focus'.
- Do a brief paragraph plan for each of these questions.
- Work through the activities in the workbook that accompanies this revision guide.
- Do not stay up late the night before the exam to do last-minute revision. If you do not know it by then, you will never know it. Instead relax, maybe get some fresh air, and have an early night.

General Test Tips

- Clear your mind, relax before you enter the exam hall.
- Read the question properly.
- Make sure you answer the question you have been set, not the one you wanted to be set.
- Write brief notes on the paper and / or highlight important words and phrases.
- Do a quick plan, using the method that suits you best.
- Address the question, showing you understand it, in your opening paragraph.
- Focus on the extracts you have been given, but show that you understand the play as a whole by making references to what happens before and after the extract.
- Always write in the present tense, as if the play is happening in front of you, unless you are answering an empathy question.
- Make sure you use quotations, but do not make them too long.
- Remember PEE (point, evidence, explanation).
- Remember you are writing about a play, written to be performed on stage. Make references to the audience.
- Make sure you give yourself enough time to comment on both extracts.
- Make sure you have a few minutes at the end to check your work.
- Enjoy writing your answer and hope that the examiner enjoys reading it.

Test Question Tips

The guidance and model answers in this section should have helped you to understand what is required to get as many marks as you can from the Shakespeare paper. But here is a recap of the key points you need to be able to demonstrate in order to get high marks. You need to...

- refer to both extracts
- include quotations from the text and explain what they mean
- show an understanding of what is going on in the extracts
- explore the focus of the question
- explain why a character behaves in a certain way
- refer to language, how characters' speech reflects the themes of the scene and how it can be interpreted on stage
- use technical terms, such as metaphor, soliloquy, where appropriate
- show you understand the main themes of play and how they are expressed in the extract.

The Writing Paper

Important Information

About the Writing Paper

- It tests your writing skills.
- It lasts for 1 hour and 15 minutes.
- There are 50 marks available.

This paper is designed to examine your skills and ability to write in different appropriate styles. There will be two tasks on this paper:

- a longer writing task that you should spend 45 minutes on, which is worth 30 marks
- a shorter writing task that you should spend 30 minutes on, which is worth 20 marks.

Each task will provide you with a theme / starting point to write about. It is up to you to allocate your time appropriately. For the longer writing task it is recommended that you spend 15 minutes planning your answer. There will be a planning page provided for you in the test. Your planning is not marked and therefore will not affect your final mark. The shorter writing task does not have planning time, although you should aim to spend about 5 minutes planning your answer.

What is Being Tested?

The test's mark scheme is based on eight assessment focuses which are used to assess different writing skills.

1. Write imaginatively, interestingly and thoughtfully. (This is called composition).
2. Use a style that is appropriate for the task and for your reader.
3. Organise your writing effectively.
4. Use paragraphs effectively.
5. Use a variety of sentence structures.
6. Use appropriate punctuation.
7. Use appropriate and effective vocabulary.
8. Use correct spelling.

These eight points cover the assessment focuses. Bearing them in mind when you are planning and writing your answer should help you to achieve the best mark possible.

About this Section of the Revision Guide

This section of the revision guide will look at the aspects you will be marked on from the assessment focuses and give you some ideas of how you can make sure your writing is suitable for the reader, as well as being interesting and varied. It will also give you pointers on how to tackle test-style questions.

The sky was purple and black, like a huge angry bruise. Huge clouds were amassing in the East like some terrible army that was about to strike. The sea was gun metal grey and waves were swelling in the water, their edges tipped with white.

The beach was deserted – no holiday makers here now – and the sand was crusted with debris from the sea: driftwood; seaweed; net and plastic bottles in an untidy, stinking heap. The only sound that could be heard was the lonely cries of the seagulls that dipped and wheeled through the darkening skies.

Sarah snuggled into her jacket and blew into her scarf for warmth; a wind had blown up and was whipping sand into her face, her eyes and her ears. She squinted against the sand and wind and trudged onwards, her body bent into the wind, her hair flying behind her like some demented flag.

She knew they would be starting to worry now, furtively glancing at the clock and counting back the hours to when she was last seen. She knew her mobile phone lay, unplugged, in a drawer in her bedroom; its silence causing angry patches to appear on her father's pale face. She knew all of these things, but she did not care.

Let them worry. Let them feel the cold pebble of fear. Let them cry, as she had done so many times in her lonely bedroom.

Sarah saw the light in the distance, the plume of smoke from the tiny chimney. Soon she would be there; soon she would be safe. She ran the last few yards along the beach, through the weather-beaten gate, up the untidy path to the sturdy wooden door. She rang the bell and the door was opened.

---

43 Spring Lane
Tiverton
Devon
EX16 9QP
Monday, 13 March 2006

Dear Mrs Smith,

I am writing to you today to voice my strong opposition to the building of a housing estate upon the local park. Although I am strongly against this proposal I do recognise that there are some important issues about the lack of housing in the town.

Firstly, if a housing estate is built on Wordsworth park where would the children play? Where would the football, rugby and cricket teams compete? Where would people exercise their dogs? There is very little green space left and if our park were to be taken away I believe that the whole town would suffer. Do you want the young to become fat and unhealthy?

However, I do appreciate that housing is a problem in the town especially for young people. But have you considered the old gas works? This derelict place is not only dangerous but an eyesore as well. Why not build some small, attractive flats that would be affordable to young people? This would clear up an unpleasant part of town, provide housing and enable us to keep our park.

In conclusion, I believe we should keep our park for all the people of our town, young and old. I recognise that the town needs housing for young people; one day I wish to buy a house in this town and will need somewhere affordable to live. But why can't these two ideas go together? I urge you to reconsider your plans and search for a new space for the housing estate.

Yours sincerely

Laura Jones

PAUL IS PICK OF THE POPS

Yesterday, local teenager Paul Jones, 16, beat thousands of hopefuls when he was chosen to go into the Pop Star House in London.

SUPER TALENT

Paul, who entered the competition last June, has been through a series of gruelling rounds to get this far and has caught the eye of Pop Star expert Kareena Twilight. Kareena has been mentoring Paul and is confident he can win the show, saying last week that he had super talent. Paul will join the nine other hopefuls in their London mansion tomorrow night to prepare for the first live show on Saturday. 'I'm excited but nervous, I want to make my family and friends proud but I think I will miss them, and Brawley of course.'

LOCAL BOY

Paul lives on the Newby Estate in Brawley and works in the kitchen at the White Hart Pub. Paul has been involved in singing for many years, taking the lead in the school's production of Oliver and has been a regular in the local theatre group's shows. Paul's Mum, Jeanette, 37, who owns the dress shop 'A Stitch in Time' on the High Street, is no stranger to publicity herself. Jeanette was Miss Brawley in 1984 and is a popular singer at the pub's karaoke evening. She said, 'I am very excited for Paul, this is all he has ever wanted to do.'

WHAT NEXT?

But will this new-found fame change Paul? Best mate, Will Green exclusively told this reporter, 'Paul won't change: he's too down to earth'. Get behind our local lad and vote for him to win!

Not all the assessment focuses are covered in both tasks. The table below shows how the assessment focuses are split between the tasks and how many marks each one is worth.

Writing Triplets

Each task will be linked to a different writing triplet from the National Curriculum. The writing triplets are...

- imagine, explore, entertain
- inform, explain, describe
- analyse, comment, review
- persuade, argue, advise.

You will have covered these at school. It is important that you have a clear idea of what is expected from each one because each triplet needs a different set of skills. As we don't know which triplets will appear in the test, it is best to revise all of them. They are all looked at in detail on p.82–90.

Assessment Focus	Longer writing task	Shorter writing task
1 Write imaginatively, interestingly and thoughtfully.	Composition and style (14 marks)	Composition and style (10 marks)
2 Use a style which is appropriate for the task and the reader.		
3 Organise your writing effectively.	Organisation and paragraphs (8 marks)	Sentence structure, organisation and paragraphs (8 marks)
4 Use paragraphs effectively.		
5 Use a variety of sentence structures.	Sentence structure and punctuation (8 marks)	
6 Use appropriate punctuation and check your work is accurate.		
7 Use appropriate and effective vocabulary.	Vocabulary	Vocabulary
8 Use correct spelling.		Spelling (4 marks)

Spelling

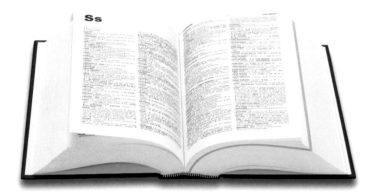

You should always try to spell your words correctly, but it is important that you pay particular attention to your **spelling** in the shorter writing task in the test as it is worth 4 marks. Look back at pieces of work that your teacher has marked to find words you have spelt incorrectly. Make a list of the correct spellings of these words and test yourself to check that you have remembered them. Here are some pairs / groups of words that often get confused…

Accept – to receive, 'I accept your gift with thanks'.
Except – without, 'all the boys except John went to town'.

Aloud – out loud, 'to check your punctuation, read your work aloud'.
Allowed – permitted, 'chewing is not allowed in the exam hall'.

Hear – you h<u>ear</u> with your <u>ears</u>, 'I can hear the music'.
Here – in this place, 'it's here'.

Its – belonging to it (no apostrophe, like his and hers), 'the cat licked its paws'.
It's – short for 'it is' (the apostrophe shows that the 'i' is missing), 'it's a long way to Tipperary'.

Lie – to rest in a horizontal position (present tense) as used in present-tense narratives, 'as I lie on my bed, watching the birds at the window…'
Lay – past tense of lie, 'last night I lay on my bed for a while'.

Lay – to set down on a surface (present tense) 'lay the table', 'hens lay eggs'.

No – opposite of 'yes', 'no, I didn't like it'.
Know – to be aware of something (present tense), 'I didn't know Michael was there'.

Now – immediately, 'I've got to go now'.

Knew – to be aware of something (past tense), 'I knew you were lying'.
New – opposite of old, 'it's a new bag'.

Passed – a verb, 'I passed all my GCSEs', 'the car passed me by'.
Past – has to be used with another verb, 'he went past on his bike.
Past – a noun indicating a previous time 'it's all in the past now'.

Practice – a noun, 'netball practice is cancelled'.
Practise – a verb, 'if you practise hard you might get into the team'.
(The same rule applies to **advice / advise**.)

Quiet – silent, 'I knew there was something wrong because the class was so quiet'.
Quite – fairly, a bit, 'the essay was quite good'.

Right – opposite of wrong, 'the right way'.
Write – what you do in a test. Someone who writes is a writer, 'she writes well'.

There – in that place, 'I'll be there soon', or 'there is', 'there are' etc.
They're – 'they are' (the apostrophe shows that the 'a' is missing) 'they're not friends'.
Their – belonging to them, 'they left their bags on the bus'.

To – towards, 'he went to bed', or part of the infinitive of a verb, 'to do', 'to think', etc.
Too – excessively, 'we had too many sweets and too much chocolate'.
Two – the number 2, 'the two bears were tired'.

We're – 'we are' (the apostrophe shows that the 'a' is missing), 'we're not sure'.
Were – to be (past tense), 'we were very cold last night'.

Where – a place, 'where am I?'.
Wear – used with clothes etc., 'I will wear my gold earrings'.

Whether – if, 'I don't know whether to go or not'.
Weather – the sun, wind, rain etc., 'the weather was terrible'.

Whose – belonging to someone, 'whose coat is on the floor?'.
Who's – short for 'who is' or 'who has', 'who's that boy over there?', 'who's dropped that coat?'.

ANSI ● abb

answer ●

action to

Punctuation

Punctuation is a very important part of any piece of writing. It helps the reader because it tells them how to read the writing. Some of the things it can tell you are…

- where a sentence starts (shown by a capital letter)
- where a sentence ends (shown by a full stop)
- which parts of sentences go together (shown by commas)
- what the tone of the writing is (shown by question marks and exclamation marks).

Here are the punctuation marks you should know, together with a brief reminder of how and when they are used.

Capital letters are used to show the start of a new sentence, or to show that a word is the name of a person or place (a pronoun), e.g. Drew Barrymore, The Statue of Liberty.

Full stops . are used to show the end of a sentence.

Commas , are used in sentences (see p.75). The comma's main functions are…

- listing – commas are used to separate items in a list, e.g. apples, bananas, pears and cherries.

- joining – they can be used with a connecting word (like 'and', 'but', 'so', etc.) to join together two sentences which can stand alone, e.g. The park bench was empty, so I sat down.
- bracketing – they are used like brackets to indicate information that could be omitted without affecting the sentence, e.g. Mr Mulvey, our favourite teacher, is getting married in June.

Question marks ? are used at the end of a direct question and at the end of a rhetorical question, e.g. Is this how it should be?

Exclamation marks ! are used to add emphasis, e.g. Help!

Colons : are used…

- before an explanation or an example, e.g. The marathon is a very long race: 26 miles!
- before a list, e.g. I got loads of presents for my birthday: a mountain bike, a Playstation 2 and loads of games.

The part before the colon needs to be a complete sentence, but the part after does not need to be.

Semi-colons ; are used to show that two sentences are closely related, e.g. The game may be cancelled; it depends on the weather. The parts before and after the semi-colon both need to be complete sentences.

Apostrophes ' are only used for two reasons:

- to show possession (ownership)
  If the owner is singular, or the word for plural owners does not end in an 's' (e.g. sheep, men, etc.) you need to add an apostrophe and an 's' to the word that indicates the owner, e.g. the cat's tail, the children's books, Miss Jones's class. When the word for the owner is plural and ends in 's', simply add an apostrophe, e.g. the cats' tails, the students' books, the princesses' dresses.
- to show omission or contraction (replacing a missing letter or letters)
  The apostrophe for omission is used mostly in speech or informal writing, e.g. shouldn't = should not, it's raining = it is raining, Mark's running away = Mark is running away.

You should try to use a range of punctuation accurately to make your meaning clear and to create particular effects. This is what will earn you top marks in the test.

Tense and Voice

Tense

The way a sentence describes an action tells you when it happened. This is particularly important in stories, because you need to know what order events happen. The three **tenses** you will use in your writing and how they are used are explained in the table below.

Tense	Used...	For example
Present tense	for an action that is happening now	I walk I am walking
Past tense	for an action that happened in the past	I walked I was walking I had walked
Future tense	for an action that will happen in the future	I will walk I will go walking I will be walking I am going to walk

Different tenses can be used in writing to create effects. For example...

- past tense can be used...
  - to tell a story, because normally the whole story has finished before you start to tell it, e.g. 'Once upon a time, there lived a princess called Beatrice...'
  - in a diary entry, e.g. 'I went round to Mark's house today and we watched zombie films all afternoon.'

- present tense is used...
  - in plays because the action is happening in front of the audience
  - to tell a story. This creates the effect that we are experiencing the action at the same time as the character, and can also create suspense, e.g. 'I am running away from my attacker, but another man dressed in black blocks the doorway in front of me. I'm trapped.'

- future tense is used to indicate something that will happen in the future and can be used in any type of writing, e.g. 'It will rain tomorrow'.

Voice

Voice refers to the way the writer relates to the reader. This depends on whether the writer chooses to tell the story from his own point of view ('I crossed the street...') or if he narrates a story as if he is observing it ('Kurt crossed the street...'). The three voices and how they are used are outlined in the table below.

Voice	Singular	Plural	When used...
First person	I, me	we, us	in a story in a letter
Second person	you (one person)	you (more than one person)	in a letter in a diary entry, e.g. 'you won't believe what happened'
Third person	he, she, it, proper names, e.g. Stacy	they	in a story in a newspaper article

In the test you need to make sure that the voice you use is suitable for the type of writing you are asked to produce. Whichever voice you choose to use, you need to make sure you stick to that voice. If you change voice halfway through it will confuse your reader. The example below is an extract from an imaginary diary entry a candidate has written. The writer is writing from the point of view of a 10-year old girl called Stacy.

Saturday 18 June 2005
Today Mum made me go into town with her and Dad and Jamie because she said we had to get new clothes because we are getting too big for the ones we are wearing now. So they all went into town. Jamie got a pair of really cool jeans. Stacy found some pretty earrings but her Mum said she couldn't have them because she's got too many.

In the example above, the writer started out in character by imagining she was Stacy, but by the end of the extract she has forgotten that she is meant to be in character and has started to write about Stacy as if she is someone else. This makes it very confusing for the reader.

Verb Forms

Verbs describe actions and are often referred to as 'doing' words, e.g. run, laugh, sing etc. We all use verbs in our sentences. However, there are special types of verbs that will help you to gain more marks if you use them in your writing.

Infinitives

The **infinitive** of a verb is formed by putting 'to' in front of the root of the verbs, e.g. 'to help'. The root is the most basic form of the verb, i.e. with no suffixes like '-ing' added. Infinitives can be used in writing to help your work sound more formal, e.g.

- *to alleviate* these problems…
- *to attach* the cord you need…
- the starting gun tells the athletes when *to run*.

Modal Verbs

Modal verbs (sometimes just called 'modals') are often used to help the main verb. Modal verbs are…

can, could, may, might, must,
ought, shall, should, will, would.

Modals can alter the tone of writing. They can be used for a variety of things:

- to make an instruction sound more polite by turning it into a question, e.g. compare 'Give the dog his dinner' with 'Can you give the dog his dinner?'
- to highlight or give emphasis to what you want to say, e.g. 'It should be easy to operate', 'It will appeal to young people'
- to introduce a suggestion, e.g. 'You could ask your teacher for help'
- to show the link between cause and effect, e.g. 'If you press the recall button, the phone will redial the number'.

Adverbs

These are used to give more information about verbs; they describe the verb. Many **adverbs** end in '-ly'. (Don't get them confused with adjectives, which describe nouns.)

- She skipped happily.
- He ran quickly.
- They sang beautifully.

Adverbs are essential in creative writing. You could write…

The cat sat on the mat, watching the birds.

But by adding adverbs, you can add more detail to the sentence so it becomes much more descriptive:

The cat sat **quietly** on the mat, **patiently** watching the birds.

You can see that by adding adverbs, sentences can be made more interesting. Where you put the adverb in the sentence can also affect the pace of the sentence:

Quietly, the cat sat on the mat, **patiently** watching the birds.

Remember if you put an adverb at the beginning of the sentence it will need a comma after it.

Sentence Length

Maintaining Interest

Examiners want you to be able to use sentences of different lengths. You must vary the length of your sentences otherwise you may bore your reader! Read the following piece of writing:

> The road was long and winding. There were huge oak trees on either side of the road. The branches creaked and swayed. There was a gathering storm. It was like human souls were trapped inside a nightmare world. There was a crack of thunder.

You can probably picture the scene it is trying to set. However, the series of short sentences breaks the flow of the text and makes it a bit boring to read. This piece of writing could be made more interesting by joining together some of the shorter sentences to vary the sentence length and by adding more descriptive words. Here is one way that it could be improved…

> The road was long and winding with huge oak trees on either side, which creaked and swayed their ancient limbs in the gathering storm as if they were humans souls trapped in a nightmare world. Suddenly, there was a crack of thunder.

The long sentence adds description and sets the pace. The second, shorter sentence creates tension and excitement. By varying your sentence structure, you not only make your writing more lively but your reader will have a much easier time understanding your meaning because you will maintain their interest.

Sentence Structure

There are different types of sentences that you should try to use in your writing: simple, compound and complex sentences. This section will help you revise these types. But whichever type of sentence you write, remember…

All sentences begin with a capital letter and end with a full stop.

There are four types of sentences – each type has a different function:

- statements are the ones used most often, e.g. Dogs like bones.
- questions are used to gain information, e.g. Does your dog like bones?
- instructions are used to tell someone to do something. They often begin with a verb, e.g. Pick up your clothes.
- exclamations are used for emphasis and use exclamation marks, e.g. Fabulous!

Simple Sentences

A **simple sentence** contains one main clause. The main clause usually has a subject, a verb and an object:

- a **subject** is a person or thing
- a **verb** is a doing word
- the **object** is the thing acted on by the verb.

Subject	Verb	Object

The cat sat on the mat.

Compound Sentences

A **compound sentence** is formed by linking two simple sentences with a connective. A connective is a joining word, such as 'and', 'but', 'then', 'or', 'so', e.g.

- I went to the shop and bought some milk.
- I went to the shop, but it was closed.
- I went to the shop, then I bought some milk.

Varying your Sentence Structure

You should try to vary your sentence structures as this will help you to gain more marks. The 'ladder' below shows a range of useful words and connectives which should help you to write varied sentences. You will earn more marks if you are able to use a range of connectives, especially the ones higher in the ladder.

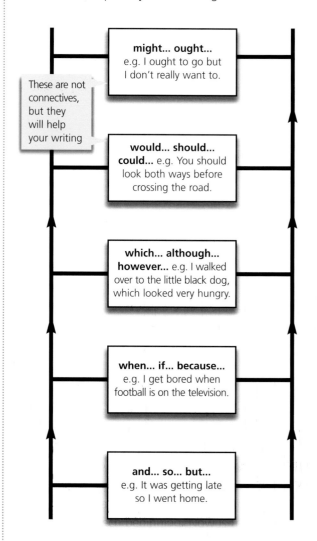

In your sentences the examiners are looking for…

- variety – can you use different types of sentences?
- clarity – are your sentences clear, do they make sense?
- accuracy – is your punctuation correct?

Complex Sentences

Complex sentences usually have subordinate clauses (sometimes called 'subclauses') and often have phrases which give further information.

The simple sentence 'the cat was sitting on the mat' can be extended by inserting additional information to turn it into a complex sentence.

Main clause   Subordinate clause

The cat, which was black with white markings, was sitting on the mat with her tiny kitten.

Subordinate clauses can be added before, in the middle or after the main clause. If you can use these, you will really impress the examiner and it will earn you more marks. The subordinate clauses are underlined in the following examples...

- <u>As I am sure you already know</u>, a new skate park has opened in Thyme Square.
- The skate park was built, <u>despite protests from local residents</u>, in just over three months.
- Davey Speed was determined to open the park, <u>even though he is only 18</u>.

Using Sentences Appropriately

You would use a different type of sentence depending on what message you need it to convey. If you were writing an advertisement for a new skate park. You might include...

- a simple sentence to give facts
  e.g. The skate park has three large ramps.
- a compound sentence to make a statement
  e.g. The park is very popular and it can get busy at weekends.
- a complex sentence to give more information about the skate park's features
  e.g. When I arrived, the coffee bar was packed with both skaters and non-skaters.

What To Do

You should alter the length and complexity of the sentences you write so they are appropriate to the subject, the audience and the purpose of the writing. Your writing should demonstrate that you can control your writing and can confidently...

- vary the lengths of your sentences appropriately
- vary your sentence structures to help develop ideas
- use different sentence structures (such as simple, compound and complex sentences) to make your meaning clear and to emphasise various points.

Paragraphs

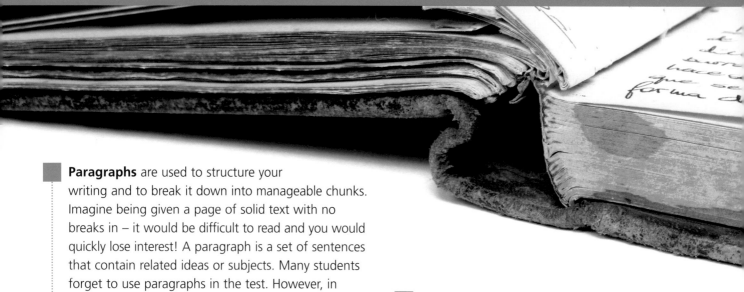

Paragraphs are used to structure your writing and to break it down into manageable chunks. Imagine being given a page of solid text with no breaks in – it would be difficult to read and you would quickly lose interest! A paragraph is a set of sentences that contain related ideas or subjects. Many students forget to use paragraphs in the test. However, in order to get higher marks you must make sure you do.

When to Use Paragraphs

Paragraphs are used to show a change in...

- time

> During the Summer Joe found he had plenty of time to help at the animal sanctuary. The Summer holidays seemed to last forever and even when he was at school the warm nights meant it was fun working outdoors with the dogs and ponies.
>
> However, when winter came, bringing the cold dark nights, Joe found he had less time to devote to the animals.

- speaker

> Fern was watching Rafferty as he struggled with his maths homework.
> "You're making a mess of that," said Fern.
> "I know," said Rafferty.

- place or person

> The classroom was dark and dingy with an old sour smell that seemed to be coming from the drains, or maybe it was coming from the new teacher.
> The playground was a different picture, bright and light with lovely green banks to roll down, a climbing frame and even a place to play football.

Remember: A paragraph is a group of sentences with shared ideas. If you change time, speaker, place or person or have a new idea, you must start a new paragraph.

Marking New Paragraphs

In the test, there are two different ways of showing that you are using a new paragraph. One way is to leave a line between paragraphs, like this...

> I believe that forcing students to wear an uncomfortable uniform is wrong.
>
> However, I realise that some people feel differently about uniform and believe its benefits outweigh its negative points.

The other way is to indent the first line of a new paragraph, like this...

> I believe that forcing students to wear an uncomfortable uniform is wrong.
>   However, I realise that some people feel differently about uniform and believe its benefits outweigh its negative points.

If you get to the end of your written test and realise you have forgotten to put your work into paragraphs, you need to show the examiner where you would have put the paragraphs. This is done by a drawing a diagonal line where the break should have been, like this...

> I believe that forcing students to wear an uncomfortable uniform is wrong. / However, I realise that some people feel differently about uniform and believe its benefits outweigh its negative points.

Some students also write NP (meaning 'new paragraph') in the margin.

Organising Your Writing

For non-fiction writing (which is basically everything except stories and poetry) there are a number of things you can do to organise your writing.

Opening and Concluding (Closing)

Opening and **concluding** paragraphs are very important when structuring your writing. The opening should make clear your intentions and the conclusion should summarise the main points. The opening and concluding paragraphs should be linked. The example below shows the first and last paragraphs of a letter written in response to an article in a school newspaper. Look at how the last paragraph refers back to the first paragraph.

> I am writing to express my views over the article which I read in the school newspaper. Though I agree there are some safety issues about the tuck shop, I do not agree with all the points that were made.
>
> [...]
>
> I do hope you will give some consideration to the views I have expressed, especially those regarding safety, and the other issues I have raised. I look forward to hearing about your final plans for the tuck shop in the near future.

Connectives

Connectives are words that link words, clauses, sentences and paragraphs and they can really help you to organise your work. Here are some connectives that you might find useful:

firstly... clearly... because... therefore... however... equally... most importantly... for example... naturally... in addition... in conclusion... finally...

Connectives can be used in a variety of ways:
- in the middle or at the beginning of a sentence, e.g. 'The television programme has been popular with young people <u>despite</u> the fact it is on after 11.00p.m.', '<u>Naturally</u> some people will say that we should be free to decide our own future.'
- to connect paragraphs, e.g. 'We believe that forcing students to wear an uncomfortable and dangerous uniform is wrong. <u>However</u>, I realise that some people feel differently about uniform and believe its benefits outweigh its negative points.'
- to open and close arguments, e.g. '<u>Firstly</u>, I would like to note that...', '<u>In</u> conclusion I feel that...'

Connectives Ladder

Look at this ladder of connectives. Start on the bottom rung and try to include all the different uses of connectives in your writing.

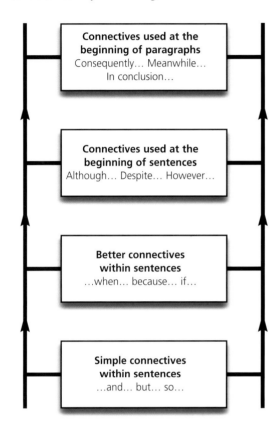

Connectives used at the beginning of paragraphs
Consequently... Meanwhile... In conclusion...

Connectives used at the beginning of sentences
Although... Despite... However...

Better connectives within sentences
...when... because... if...

Simple connectives within sentences
...and... but... so...

Audience and Purpose

Your ability to compose a piece of writing to create a specific effect is what will gain you most marks. The examiner is looking for two things:
- a piece of writing that is appropriate to task, purpose and audience
- an imaginative, interesting and thoughtful piece of writing.

You need to consider...
- who your audience is
- the purpose of the writing.

Audience

Your **audience** is whoever the piece of writing is going to be read by. You need to make sure you write appropriately for your audience. This includes choosing a subject that will interest them, using language and specialist terms (if any) that they are familiar with, and presenting the text in an appropriate format. The table below includes some audiences you might be asked to write for together with some suggestions as to how you could write to attract and maintain their interest.

Audience	Use...
Teenagers	informal language, slang terms, catchy phrases, short sentences, smaller sections of text to maintain interest
Football fans	informal language, slang terms
The local council	formal language, structured and organised sentences, probably wouldn't include images
Teachers	formal language, no spelling mistakes!
Children	basic language, short sentences

Purpose

You also need to bear in mind why you are writing. You should make sure you use a style appropriate to the **purpose** of the writing. In the exam, the purpose of a piece of writing will be one of the following:
- to imagine, explore, entertain
- to inform, explain, describe
- to persuade, argue, advise
- to analyse, comment, review.

The questions in the exam may not include the words exactly as they appear in the list above, so look for the main part of the word, e.g. ...
- 'use your imagination to...' instead of imagine
- 'write an informative article about...' instead of inform
- 'write a descriptive account of...' instead of describe
- 'use your persuasive skills to...' instead of persuade
- 'write an analysis of...' instead of analyse, etc.

These purposes are each looked at on p.82–90 to help you revise the features usually associated with each type of writing. An example question and annotated model answer are also provided so you can get a better idea of what you are expected to do in the test.

Format and Language

Format

There are many different **formats** you could be asked to write in the style of in a test. The table below features some formats and the features / layouts that could be used for each one.

Format	Features of layout
Story	paragraphs of texts, usually broken into chapters
Holiday brochure	small chunks of descriptive text
Newspaper article	short paragraphs, main facts of story in opening sentence, rest of article gives more detail
Letter	your address, their address, the date, greeting (Dear Mr Smith), the main body of the letter, signing off (yours sincerely)
Leaflet	small chunks of text

Language

The purpose of the writing, the audience it is intended for and the format of the writing all affect the **language** and **vocabulary** that you will use.

To make your language suitable for a specific audience you need to use the correct register. The register is the tone of voice and the level of formality you use, i.e. addressing a letter to someone you have not met using 'Dear Sir / Madam' rather than abbreviating their name, e.g. 'Hiya Kev'. It also relates to the vocabulary you use, e.g. using slang and specialist football terms would be appropriate for a football fans magazine, but would be completely unsuitable in a letter to the local council.

Format	Features of Language
Story	descriptive language to describe characters, action and places, includes characters' speech
Holiday brochure	positive, descriptive language to 'sell' the destination
Newspaper article	emotive and sensational language, alliteration (especially in headings), puns, rhyme and rhetorical questions
Letter of complaint	formal language, facts
Charity Leaflet	bullets points, descriptions of those who need help, rhetorical questions, request for help

FLAP

This is a handy mnemonic to help you remember all the things you need to consider when you are writing: **F**ormat **L**anguage **A**udience **P**urpose

Approaching Test Questions

A Test-style Question

Now that we have covered all the skills necessary to do well in the test, it is time to look at how to tackle the test paper.

In the test you will have to write one short piece of writing and one long piece. You should try to divide your time appropriately between the two tasks – it is no good spending the majority of the time writing a fantastic piece for the longer task and only leaving yourself a few minutes for the shorter task.

You should aim to spend 45 minutes on the longer writing task, including 15 minutes to plan your answer. A planning page will be provided for you. Your planning is not marked so it will not affect your final mark. The planning page is usually divided into sections. You may use these sections or you may wish to plan in a different way.

Try to leave yourself 30 minutes for the shorter writing task. You should try to spend about 5 minutes of this on planning your answer as this will help you to write an organised and well-structured piece which will help you get higher grades.

What to Do in the Test

Always make sure you carefully read the question that is set: it will give you all the information you need. Read through the question and underline the key words. If it helps, write down the FLAP mnemonic and fill it in. The first thing you should think about is the purpose of the writing so look out for the word that tells you why you are writing the piece. Then look at who you are writing for (audience) and the format you have been asked to write in, and finally think about the language that you should use.

Below is a test-style question like you might get in the test. It has been annotated by the candidate to pick out the important points.

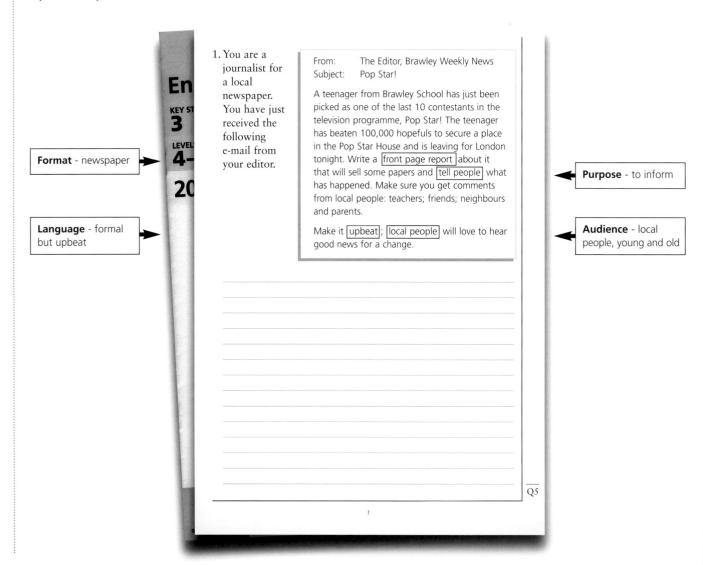

Format - newspaper

Language - formal but upbeat

1. You are a journalist for a local newspaper. You have just received the following e-mail from your editor.

From: The Editor, Brawley Weekly News
Subject: Pop Star!

A teenager from Brawley School has just been picked as one of the last 10 contestants in the television programme, Pop Star! The teenager has beaten 100,000 hopefuls to secure a place in the Pop Star House and is leaving for London tonight. Write a front page report about it that will sell some papers and tell people what has happened. Make sure you get comments from local people: teachers; friends; neighbours and parents.

Make it upbeat; local people will love to hear good news for a change.

Purpose - to inform

Audience - local people, young and old

Planning Your Answer

The test paper will have a page for you to plan your answer on. It may be divided up into sections with headings for you to think about. You can use these sections or choose to organise your writing another way.

There are many different methods of planning you can use including…
- making lists
- drawing spider diagrams
- using symbols to organise your thoughts.

You can find examples of each of these in the Shakespeare section. Experiment with different methods of planning to see which one works best for you, e.g. you could brainstorm your ideas using a spider diagram, but don't forget to number your points so you know what order you will tackle them in when you come to write your piece. This will help you to structure your writing.

Whichever method you use, remember to think about what you will include in each section. You need to have a structure: opening, middle, conclusion.

If you were planning what to write for the question on the previous page, your plan might look something like this…

First paragraph – main facts – local boy Paul Jones, 16, beat thousands of hopefuls, etc.

Main body – more information…
- recent show information
- Paul's singing history
- where he lives
- quotes from family

Concluding paragraph – What does the future hold for Paul? Will he change? Information about how to vote.

Writing to Imagine, Explore and Entertain

Writing to imagine, explore and entertain is usually associated with creative writing. The key features of this sort of writing are…

- stories / plot
- characters
- descriptions
- use of literary techniques (see p.16).

Each style or type of writing has conventions, rules and devices that govern how it should be written. When writing stories, many students fall into the trap of writing action-led stories. Don't forget to describe characters and settings and include speech. Try to use varied vocabulary as well to keep the reader's interest. And plan your structure before you start writing – if you can't remember your point how do you expect the reader to be able to follow your logic? Try to include features to make your creative writing more interesting.

Vary your **vocabulary** – use a range of words rather than repeating the same ones and try to be clear, e.g. 'mournful', 'miserable' and 'melancholy' all mean 'sad' but in different degrees.

Use **imagery** – you can create vivid images with language and they don't just have to be things you can see. Remember there are five senses – sight, hearing, smell, touch and taste – try to appeal to all of them.

Devices are the tools which help us create images. Here are some you could use:

- simile – a comparison using 'like' or 'as', e.g. the ruined buildings looked <u>like</u> broken hearts

- metaphor – a direct comparison, e.g. the ruined buildings <u>were</u> broken hearts…
- alliteration – repetition of sound at the beginning of words, e.g. <u>b</u>ig <u>b</u>alls <u>b</u>ounced
- assonance – repetition of sound in the middle of words, e.g. the v<u>a</u>le b<u>a</u>de me goodbye
- consonance – the repetition of sound at the end of words, e.g. shak<u>ing</u>, rattl<u>ing</u>, roll<u>ing</u>
- personification – giving inanimate objects / animals human qualities, e.g. the corn whispered in the breeze
- onomatopoeia – words that sound like their action, e.g. buzz, swish, hiss and plop
- rule of three – when three adjectives are used or something is repeated three times, e.g. the monster came on great, resilient, striding legs.

Refer back to p.16 (in the Reading Paper section) for more information on these and other literary techniques.

The **structure** of the writing / paragraph / sentence can affect the way the text is read. Short sentences and paragraphs can be used when you want to draw attention to something, whereas long sentences or paragraphs can be used for detailed descriptions, or to delay a discovery and so prolong the suspense.

Long vowel sounds can be used to slow the pace and soften the sound, e.g. the clown was downcast and feeling rather melancholy. Short, sharp words, often monosyllabic (one syllable) quicken the pace, e.g. 'The race was fast: at full pelt. To win was all'.

Question and Model Answer

En...
KEY ST...
3
LEVEL'
4–
20

5. Write a [description] of a beach to include in a [novel] for [teenagers]. You may want to think about...
   – what time of day and year it is. For example, is the beach busy with holiday makers or cold and deserted?
   – what happens on the beach
   – who is on the beach.

Format
- novel
Language
- description
Audience
- teenagers
Purpose
- to entertain

The sky was purple and black, like a huge angry bruise. Huge clouds were amassing in the East like some terrible army that was about to strike. The sea was gun metal grey and waves were swelling in the water, their edges tipped with white.

The beach was deserted – no holiday makers here now – and the sand was crusted with debris from the sea: driftwood; seaweed; net and plastic bottles in an untidy, stinking heap. The only sound that could be heard was the lonely cries of the seagulls that dipped and wheeled through the darkening skies.

Sarah snuggled into her jacket and blew into her scarf for warmth; a wind had blown up and was whipping sand into her face, her eyes and her ears. She squinted against the sand and wind and trudged onwards, her body bent into the wind, her hair flying behind her like some demented flag.

She knew they would be starting to worry now, furtively glancing at the clock and counting back the hours to when she was last seen. She knew her mobile phone lay, unplugged, in a drawer in her bedroom; its silence causing angry patches to appear on her father's pale face. She knew all of these things, but she did not care.

Let them worry. Let them feel the cold pebble of fear. Let them cry, as she had done so many times in her lonely bedroom.

Sarah saw the light in the distance, the plume of smoke from the tiny chimney. Soon she would be there; soon she would be safe. She ran the last few yards along the beach, through the weather-beaten gate, up the untidy path to the sturdy wooden door. She rang the bell and the door was opened.

(5 marks) | Q5

5

1
- Sets the scene.
- Includes a variety of visual imagery including simile and metaphor.
- Military images create a mood of danger.

2
- Correct and effective use of colon and semi-colon.
- Sensory images.
- Uses long vowel sounds in the last sentence.

3
- Introduction of character.
- Rule of three.
- Simile.

4
- Focus moves to her parents worrying.
- Rule of three – repetition in sentence structure.

5
- Rule of three – repetition of sentence structure.
- Simile and thermal imagery to convey a strong feeling.

6
- Repetition of sentence structure.
- Range of adjectives used.

Writing to Inform, Explain and Describe

Writing to inform, explain and describe is usually associated with newspaper articles, leaflets, brochures and guidebooks. The key characteristics of this kind of writing are…

- giving information
- explaining how to do something
- describing an event.

Whatever style you are writing in, the tips from the previous pages are useful. Varying your language and using a range of devices to create images will help to maintain your reader's interest whatever you are writing. A typical format associated with this type of writing is newspaper articles. Their features include…

- headlines
- subheadings
- first paragraph
- rest of the article.

Headlines use a range of devices to catch the reader's attention, such as…

- dramatic, e.g. Wall of death!
- pun, e.g. Parking mad
- rhetorical questions, e.g. Do you want to die like this?
- rhyme, e.g. Fame game shame
- alliteration, e.g. Granny gets groovy groceries!

Subheadings are used to highlight the key points made in the article. They also help to break up the text.

The **first paragraph** contains the key facts of the story in less than 25 words.

The **rest of the article** adds more information and detail to the initial paragraph. A story about an accident or natural disaster may focus on one 'victim' to evoke the reader's sympathy.

If you have to write a newspaper article, organise the facts / ideas into a logical order which makes sense to you. Then pick out the main details; these will form your first sentence or paragraph.

Other features of newspaper articles include…

- the past tense (the story has already happened)
- formal language
- sensational, emotive or persuasive language
- people's full names and age
- quotations or reported speech from victims, experts, eyewitnesses. Their relevance to the story is usually included, e.g. 'Joe Smith, 23, who lived next door, said…'

Question and Model Answer

1. You are a journalist for a local newspaper. You have just received the following e-mail from your editor.

> From: The Editor, Brawley Weekly News
> Subject: Pop Star!
>
> A teenager from Brawley School has just been picked as one of the last 10 contestants in the television programme, Pop Star! The teenager is leaving for London tonight and has beaten 100,000 hopefuls to secure a place in the Pop Star House. Write a front page report about it that will sell some papers and tell people what has happened. Make sure you get comments from local people: teachers; friends; neighbours and parents. Make it upbeat; local people will love to hear good news for a change.

Format
- front page report
Language
- sensational, upbeat
Audience
- local people
Purpose
- to inform

PAUL IS PICK OF THE POPS

Yesterday, local teenager Paul Jones, 16, beat thousands of hopefuls when he was chosen to go into the Pop Star House in London.

SUPER TALENT

Paul, who entered the competition last June, has been through a series of gruelling rounds to get this far and has caught the eye of Pop Star expert Kareena Twilight. Kareena has been mentoring Paul and is confident he can win the show, saying last week that he had super talent. Paul will join the nine other hopefuls in their London mansion tomorrow night to prepare for the first live show on Saturday. 'I'm excited but nervous, I want to make my family and friends proud but I think I will miss them, and Brawley of course.'

LOCAL BOY

Paul lives on the Newby Estate in Brawley and works in the kitchen at the White Hart Pub. Paul has been involved in singing for many years, taking the lead in the school's production of *Oliver* and has been a regular in the local theatre group's shows. Paul's Mum, Jeanette, 37, who owns the dress shop 'A Stitch in Time' on the High Street, is no stranger to publicity herself. Jeanette was Miss Brawley in 1984 and is popular at the pub's karaoke evening. She said, 'I am very excited for Paul, this is all he has ever wanted to do.'

WHAT NEXT?

But will this new-found fame change Paul? Best mate, Will Green exclusively told this reporter, 'Paul won't change: he's too down to earth'.

Get behind our local lad and vote for him to win!

Q5

1

1
- Alliterative headline.
- Who, what, where and when in under 25 words.

2
- Subheadline draws the reader in.
- Complex sentence used.
- Reported speech – not in speech marks.
- Includes additional information about the competition, then goes on to give local information.

3
- More background information provided.
- Direct quotes from family and friends are in speech marks.

4
- Rhetorical question adds excitement.
- The word 'exclusively' makes the report sound special.
- Ends on a positive request for the locals to support him.

Writing to Analyse, Comment and Review

Writing to analyse, comment and review is usually associated with newspaper or magazine reviews of books, films, games, etc.

Writing to analyse requires you to consider and judge information and viewpoints.

Writing to review requires you to give your viewpoint, usually of something like a TV programme, concert or film.

Writing to comment involves giving your viewpoint and reasons for it, but you may also need to take others' views into account and present a balanced argument.

All three of these types of writing mean that you must...
• present a balanced analysis
• take into account evidence and opinions
• justify your viewpoint with evidence.

Writing to analyse, comment and review means taking information and analysing the positive and negative aspects of it, and deciding on how it measures up, just as reviewing means watching a film or reading a book and giving your views on it. Whatever your purpose, you will need to use evaluative language.

You must also make sure you organise your writing. Remember to have an opening paragraph, a middle section and a closing paragraph, e.g.
• in the first paragraph, you may decide to give information about what you are reviewing
• in the middle section you may focus on the positive points, then go on to discuss the negative points
• in the closing paragraph you would give your judgement and give your reasons for it, based on what you have written in the middle section.

The table below includes some positive and negative words that you may find useful when writing to analyse, comment or review.

Positive Words		Negative Words	
effective	sensible	insufficient	failure
invaluable	useful	inadequate	weak
worthwhile	worked	ineffective	useless
excellent	helpful	didn't work	unhelpful
very good	valuable	unsuccessful	abysmal
adequate	suitable	lacking	unsuitable
surprising	essential	limited	deficient

Question and Model Answer

1. You are a manager at a mobile phone company. You and your team are developing a new type of phone. Write a letter to your Managing Director that analyses the successes and failures of the project so far.

En
KEY ST
3
LEVEL
4-
20

Format
- letter
Language
- standard formal English
Audience
- Managing Director
Purpose
- to analyse

Dear Managing Director,

As you already know, the TZ3000 is a new generation mobile phone that incorporates Diamond chip technology to make it the quickest and smartest mobile phone yet.

The team and I are very happy with the technology as it enables the phone to have a wide range of functions such as: Wireless internet, video messaging, high-quality photo and the usual clear voice communication function.

However, the optional portable keyboard was a disaster. At first we made it very small so that it could roll up and fit in your pocket but the key size was too small and people kept hitting the wrong keys. In order to update this, we have included a laser light function that projects a virtual keyboard from the phone. The user can make the keys as large or small as they please and this is proving popular with our trial groups.

The casing was another difficulty that we had to overcome. We decided that silver was very overdone so we have opted for a matt black case which made the phone look very stylish but we found that many people found them difficult to see, particularly women who keep them in their handbags. We decided to include a blue thread through the black which enables the owner to see it more clearly but still makes the look very stylish.

I hope you find this analysis useful. The team and I are looking forward to your comments.

Yours faithfully

Julie Mc Bean

Q5

1
- Formal opening – addressing a superior.
- Explains what report is about.
- Uses technical terms to give authenticity.

2
- Lists features of phone.
- Infinitives used.

3
- Connective used at start of paragraph.
- Negative vocabulary used to discuss a problem they experienced.
- Vocabulary becomes more positive to discuss how they overcame the problems.

4
- Another problem is discussed.
- Again how the problem was resolved is focused on.

5
- Short business-like concluding sentence.
- Appropriate sign off used.

Writing to Persuade, Argue and Advise

Writing to persuade, argue and advise is usually associated with letters, speeches and presentations. This type of writing is usually characterised by…

- expressing opinions
- presenting a balanced view
- discrediting the other opinion
- being polite but convincing.

Writing to Argue / Persuade

Here is a mnemonic to help you. When you are trying to argue or persuade you need to **PERFORM**!

P - Personal address to involve the reader
E - Emotive language and strong ending
R - Rhetorical questions and repetition
F - Facts and formal tone
O - Opening statement to grab audience's attention
R - Rule of three
M - Markers or connectives to shape your writing

In this type of writing you should…

- state your opinions, e.g. 'I feel / I think / I consider…'
- link your paragraphs, e.g. 'A further consideration must be…'
- present a balanced view, e.g. 'On the other hand…'
- be polite but convincing, e.g. 'I understand your objections…'
- give the alternative view, e.g. 'Some people have said that…'
- discredit the other opinion, e.g. 'This is misleading…'
- introduce evidence, e.g. '*The Guardian* recently published an article on…'

Writing to Advise

Writing to advise means you take on the role of the expert. You need to…

- give clear advice, e.g. 'Follow these three simple steps…'
- keep in role, e.g. 'It is my professional opinion that…'
- include modals verbs, e.g. can, will, shall, may, could, would, should, might, must, ought
- be informal but polite, e.g. 'Get your friends to help you…'
- explain the options, e.g. 'If this doesn't work then…'
- encourage and motivate the reader, e.g. 'You can do this…'

If you write a speech you should make sure it…

- is well organised
- is written to be spoken out loud to an audience
- uses language and devices to grab the audience's attention, such as, imagery; repetition of words, phrases, structures, rhythms; emotive language; rhetorical questions; rule of three.

On page 90 you will find some suggestions of useful phrases that you could use in your writing to make it sound more formal.

Question and Model Answer

1. You are an Agony Aunt and you have received the following letter in your post bag. Write a [letter] of [advice] to be published in next week's magazine. Remember to use the tips on the previous page to help you. Remember in your answer to…
   - sum up how you see the situation
   - try and see all sides of the story
   - give some practical advice.

Hello,

I am [13 years] old and I started a new school last September. My new friends mess about in class and my teachers say that my work is suffering. My dad has grounded me until my grades improve. I did OK at my last school but I am no brain box. My grades were really bad in the last exams and I found everything too hard.

Yours worried.

Format
- letter
Language
- informal but authoritative
Audience
- teenagers
Purpose
- to advise

Dear Jonathan,

Starting a new school is a difficult time for anyone. It's hard to make new friends, settle into a new routine and keep up with your school work. I am not surprised that you are finding it difficult to get the right balance. Things may seem bad at the moment, but don't worry, there are a number of things that you can do.

Firstly, talk to your new friends, explain to them that you want to settle down and work in class. If they are true friends they will understand. If not, maybe it is time to find some new friends. I appreciate that this is not an easy thing to do but you could talk to your form teacher, maybe you could be moved to a different table where you can make new friends, or you could join a club or team.

Secondly, you must maintain your academic standards whilst you are at school. I have already mentioned not talking to your friends in class. Another thing you can do is make sure you put time aside for homework. It won't hurt!

Finally, you must speak to your parents or another adult you can trust and explain how worried you are. Trust me you will feel much better once you have talked your problems through. Explain how hard you are finding settling in and try and come to a compromise with them: if you agree to work harder your parents may give you some freedom at the weekend. Your parents are obviously worried about you and they are worried because they care.

Q5

1

1
- Reassures the reader and sums up the situation.
- Use of modal verbs suggests possibilities.

2
- Offers advice about what he could do.
- Reminds him there are other people who can help him.

3
- Deals logically with the next point.

4
- Uses logical connectives to structure the piece.
- Uses a variety of sentences structures.
- Encourages talk with adults, tries to see both sides of the situation and reassures the teenager that his parents care.

Writing to Persuade, Argue and Advise

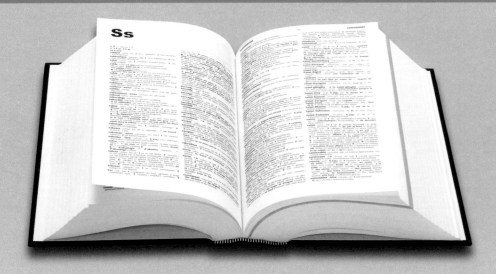

Here are some useful phrases to include if you are writing to **persuade, argue and advise**. These phrases will help your writing to sound more formal, but you don't need to memorise them all. Choose a few that you are comfortable using (and make sure you know what they mean) and use them appropriately.

Writing to Argue or Persuade

Stating your opinions:
- I feel / I think / I consider…
- It is my belief that…
- It is my considered opinion that…
- In my opinion…
- I am convinced that…

Links between paragraphs:
- Firstly, secondly, in addition, …
- A further consideration must be…
- Similarly, …

Presenting a balanced view:
- However, …
- On the other hand, …
- Nevertheless, …

Being polite but convincing:
- Clearly some people will have opposing views, but I believe…
- I understand your objections…
- I am sure you will agree that…

Giving the alternative view:
- Some people have said that…
- Some / many people believe that…
- It is widely believed that…

Discrediting the other opinion:
- Clearly, this is not true…
- However, this is not the case…
- This is simply wrong…
- This is misleading…

Introducing evidence:
- It has come to my attention that…
- A recent survey in the school newspaper found that…
- *The Guardian* recently published an article on…

Writing to Advise

Giving clear advice:
- You only need to follow these three steps…
- The first thing to do is…
- The next step…
- Finally, …

Keeping in role:
- It is my professional opinion that…
- Many young people come to me for advice…

Using informal and polite phrases:
- Get your friends to help you…
- Good luck…
- Don't panic…

Giving options:
- You could talk to your parents or another adult…
- Alternatively…
- If this doesn't work then…

Encouraging and motivating:
- Things may seem bad but don't worry…
- You can do this…
- You can be successful if you…
- I believe we can achieve anything…

Test Tips

Now you should be fully prepared for anything you may be asked to write in the test. If you are unsure about any aspects of the test or what you have read, ask your teacher or one of your parents to explain them to you. Older brothers and sisters can also come in handy!

To get the most from this revision guide, work through the companion workbook. You should also practise writing in different formats.

Before you enter the test hall, try to clear your mind and relax. Then remember these tips to help you through the test.

Read the Questions Carefully

This may sound obvious but it is the most important thing to remember! The questions will give you all the information you will need to be able to write your answer. Read through the question a couple of times, highlighting the words that tell you about what you need to include in your answer. So look out for…

- format – what are you being asked to produce?
- audience – who is it for?
- purpose – what is it for?
- language – what type of language would be suitable?

Plan Your Answer

You should aim to spend about 15 minutes planning your answer to the longer question, and about 5 minutes planning your answer to the shorter question. Use whichever method of planning you are most comfortable with – making notes in lists, using a spider diagram, making a paragraph plan, etc. Although your planning is not marked, it is useful to produce a detailed plan as it will help to guide you when you write your answer, and this should help to prevent panic setting in!

Check Your Answer

Give yourself a couple of minutes to read over your answers at the end of the test.

Finally, good luck!

Glossary

Adjective a word that describes a noun

Adverb a word that describes a verb

Aside a line spoken by a character to the audience which is not intended for the other characters to hear

Audience whoever the play / writing is going to be watched / read by

Character can refer to either 1) a character (person) in a play or 2) what a person is like

Clause a part of a sentence which contains a subject and a verb

Complex sentence a sentence containing one main clause and one subordinate clause

Compound sentence two simple sentences linked with a connective

Connective words that can link words, clauses, sentences and paragraphs

Context the circumstances or historical period in which something is set

Device a literary 'tool' used to create a particular effect

Direct (what a director does) to influence the way / mood / direction of a play

Emphasis an extra stress on certain words to highlight their importance

Fiction literature written about imaginary people and events

Genre a category of writing

Infinitive a verb formed when 'to' is put in front of the root, i.e. to go

Modal verb can only be used with other verbs to help the main verb

Mood / atmosphere an effect created by the use of language

Morals individual's perception of what is right and wrong

Motivation the reason why a character is acting the way that they do

Narrative viewpoint how the person telling the story sees things

Narrator the person who is telling the story

Non-fiction literature written about facts, real-life events

Noun a naming word

Object the 'thing' that is acted on by the verb

PEE Point, Evidence, Explanation

Phrase a fragment of a sentence; does not have to contain a verb

Poetry words that have been written into verse usually with a rhyme or rhythm

Prose ordinary writing, i.e. not verse

Punctuation the marks used in text to clarify meaning, separate sentences, indicate speech etc.

Purpose the reason why the text has been written, e.g. to advise, entertain, etc.

Simple sentence a sentence with one clause

Soliloquy a speech made by a character directly to the audience which expresses their real thoughts

Stage direction an instruction written as part of a play

Status how important someone is

Style the way the author communicates to the audience

Subject a person or thing

Subordinate clause provides additional information to a sentence (can be removed from a sentence without altering its meaning)

Tense used to show the time at which something happened – past, present or future

Theme an idea that is a recurring element in a literary work

Tone the attitude conveyed by the writing

Verb a doing (action) word

Vocabulary the range and type of words used

Notes

Index

Picture Credits

Every effort has been made to contact the holders of copyright material, but if any have been inadvertently overlooked, the Publishers will be pleased to make the necessary arrangements at the first opportunity.

The authors and publisher would like to thank everyone who contributed images to this book:

p.2 ©iStockphoto.com / Stephen Boks
p.4 Qualifications and Curriculum Authority
p.6 Qualifications and Curriculum Authority
p.7 *The Diary of Anne Frank* edited by Otto H. Frank and Miriam Pressler courtesy of Penguin Books
p.7 DEFRA
p.7 ©Bill Bryson *The Lost Continent* by Bill Bryson, published by Black Swan, a division of Transworld Publishers. All rights reserved.
p.12 ©iStockphoto.com / Graeme Purdy
p.14 ©iStockphoto.com / Fernando Caldito Lop
p.18 *The Shoemaker's Holiday* by Thomas Dekker courtesy of A & C Black (Publishers) Limited
p.19 ©iStockphoto.com / Rui Vale Sousa
p.20 *McSweeney's Mammoth Treasury of Thrilling Tales* edited by Michael Chabon courtesy of Hamish Hamilton, an imprint of Penguin Books
p.20 *Bridget Jones's Diary* by Helen Fielding courtesy of Picador, an imprint of MacMillan
p.20 *The Diary of Anne Frank* edited by Otto H. Frank and Miriam Pressler courtesy of Penguin Books
p.20 *Pol Pot The History of a Nightmare* by Philip Short courtesy of John Murray (Publishers) A division of Hodder Headline
p.21 ©iStockphoto.com / Lukasz Janicki
p.22 www.oxfam.org.uk/atwork/emerg/wateremg/html © Oxfam GB Reproduced by permission
p.22 DEFRA
p.23 ©iStockphoto.com / fanelie rosier
p.24 Qualifications and Curriculum Authority
p.24 ©iStockphoto.com / Andrzej Burak
p.27 Qualifications and Curriculum Authority
p.28 ©iStockphoto.com / Jillian Pond
p.29 Qualifications and Curriculum Authority
p.30 ©iStockphoto.com / Dainis Derics
p.30 ©iStockphoto.com / Lance Bellers
p.31 Qualifications and Curriculum Authority
p.32 ©iStockphoto.com / Laurie Knight
p.33 Qualifications and Curriculum Authority
p.38 Royal Shakespeare Company
p.39 ©iStockphoto.com / Duncan Walker
p.40 Qualifications and Curriculum Authority

p.43 Royal Shakespeare Company
p.44 *William Shakespeare (1564-1616)* courtesy of the National Portrait Gallery, London.
p.46 Qualifications and Curriculum Authority
p.49 Royal Shakespeare Company
p.50 ©iStockphoto.com / Paulus Rusyanto
p.51 ©iStockphoto.com / Roro Fernandez
p.54 Qualifications and Curriculum Authority
p.57 Royal Shakespeare Company
p.58 Royal Shakespeare Company
p.63 Royal Shakespeare Company
p.64 ©iStockphoto.com / Andres Rodriguez
p.70 ©iStockphoto.com / Christine Balderas
p.72 ©iStockphoto.com / Tina Rencelj
p.73 ©iStockphoto.com / Duncan Walker
p.74 ©iStockphoto.com / Duncan Walker
p.75 ©iStockphoto.com
p.76 ©iStockphoto.com / Alex Bramwell
p.77 ©iStockphoto.com / Christine Balderas
p.78 ©iStockphoto.com / Aaron Kohr
p.79 Funway Holidays International Inc. (www.funwayholidays.co.uk)
p.79 www.oxfam.org.uk/whatnew/press/ethiopia1.html © Oxfam GB Reproduced by permission
p.80 Qualifications and Curriculum Authority
p.81 ©iStockphoto.com / Lise Gagne
p.82 ©iStockphoto.com / Clayton Hansen
p.83 Qualifications and Curriculum Authority
p.84 ©iStockphoto.com / Kyle Maass
p.85 Qualifications and Curriculum Authority
p.86 ©iStockphoto.com / Marcos Paternoster
p.87 Qualifications and Curriculum Authority
p.88 ©iStockphoto.com / Henk van Mierlo
p.89 Qualifications and Curriculum Authority
p.91 ©iStockphoto.com / Laurence Gough